IMAGES
of America

NEW JERSEY
FOREST FIRE SERVICE

INSTRUCTIONS

For Township and District Firewardens.

LOOKOUTS.

Have a lookout or observation tower near your home from which you can see the smoke of a fire as soon as it starts. A tall tree on high ground, with a ladder fastened to it, will serve well. Three or four such lookouts scattered over your district will help you to find a fire. When the woods are dry, watch sharply for signs of fire, and find out what causes every smoke.

HORSE AND WAGON AND SHOVELS.

Have a horse and light wagon always ready in the danger season. The wagon should be strong enough to carry six men. Keep it greased.

If you use shovels in fighting fires, keep them sharp. Have a place for them under cover, and keep them in their place, to prevent loss of precious time when a fire breaks out.

GOING TO THE FIRE.

When a fire starts, lose no time in getting to it. Minutes at first are worth hours afterwards. Go with three men at once rather than wait for six.

Don't wait for meals. Have the meals sent after you and put the cost in your bill.

But before starting, send off a messenger for more men, if you need them. In serious cases telephone or telegraph the State Firewarden.

AT THE FIRE.

Upon arriving at the fire, set your men to work immediately where you are. Then go yourself with all speed along the fire line until you have ascertained the extent of the fire and the general situation. THEN DECIDE:

Where your men can accomplish the most. Whether to send for more men. Whether you must back fire.

PUT THE FIRE OUT!

When the fire is subdued keep a patrol moving along the fire line until you are sure that it is out. Make a lookout tree for him, if necessary, so that he can see above the tops of other trees and catch the first trace of smoke.

In the early morning of the day after the fire watch carefully for smoke, as the dew dries off and the wind springs up.

When patrolling, put out every smoking ember. Run no risks. Spare no pains. Put the fire completely out, then it will stay out.

MISCELLANEOUS.

Prepare a list of "helpers"—men who have agreed to fight fire when called upon to do so.

Carefully keep your badge; wear it when on duty and return it to the State Firewarden when your term of office expires. Take good care of all State property in your possession. The State Firewarden is held responsible for all equipment and keeps a list of all property issued to each warden.

If a fire gets beyond your control, immediately notify the State Firewarden by telegraph or telephone, so that he can summon help "from surrounding townships," as the law provides.

Post these instructions where you can refer to them.

T. P. PRICE,
February 1, 1908   STATE FIREWARDEN.

One of the state firewarden's responsibilities is to issue instructions to employees in carrying out the mission of the forest fire service. This February 1, 1908, poster listed instructions to be followed by township firewardens and the district firewardens appointed by them. Each municipality that was provided forest fire protection coverage by the forest fire service was required to appoint a township firewarden who was responsible for carrying out the duties of the forest fire service. Theophilus Price, whose name appears on the bottom of the instruction form, was New Jersey's first state firewarden, serving from 1906 through 1910.

On the cover: Section forest firewarden William Hagerthy and a firefighter test the pump of a Dodge WM Power Wagon off-road engine in this 1949 photograph. (Courtesy of New Jersey Forest Fire Service's Archives.)

IMAGES
of America

NEW JERSEY
FOREST FIRE SERVICE

Section Forest Firewardens of Division B

ARCADIA
PUBLISHING

Copyright © 2006 by Section Forest Firewardens of Division B
ISBN 978-1-5316-2750-8

Published by Arcadia Publishing
Charleston, South Carolina

Library of Congress Catalog Card Number: 2006921285

For all general information contact Arcadia Publishing at:
Telephone 843-853-2070
Fax 843-853-0044
E-mail sales@arcadiapublishing.com
For customer service and orders:
Toll-Free 1-888-313-2665

Visit us on the Internet at www.arcadiapublishing.com

CONTENTS

ACKNOWLEDGMENTS

The Section Forest Firewardens of Division B would like to thank the New Jersey Forest Fire Service for allowing many exceptional photographs to be utilized from the forest fire service's photographic archives for use in this book. Maris Gabliks and John Reith are to be commended for coordinating the development and design of this book, researching historic information, as well as collecting photographs and information from many individuals across New Jersey. Finally, the following people all helped contribute stories, photographs, and varied historical information for inclusion in this book. These people all helped make this book a success. They include Ken Badger Sr., Ken Badger Jr., Jim Barresi, Eileen Bethanis, Gary Burton, Ken Clark, Willie Cirone, Skip Danielson, Bob Dennis, Peter Draghi, Kevin Drake, Jim Dunn, Bill Edwards, Rich Errickson Jr., John Flyntz, Bill Fox, Robert Goff, Ricky Haines, Dave Harrison, Henry Hasselhan, Steve Holmes, Tom Horner, Joe Hughes, Chris Irick, Bill Lance, Glenn Liepe, Mike Mangum, Shirley O'Neill, Jim Petrini, Tom Philhower Jr., Harold Ryan, Ed Schoonmaker, Ed Seifert, Nick Skowronski, Horace Somes, Bob Spears, Whitey Swartz, Tom Tolska, John Wimberg, and Bob Wolff.

—Maris G. Gabliks and John H. Rieth
Section Forest Firewardens of Division B
Book Committee Project Leaders:

INTRODUCTION

The photograph on the cover of this book begins to tell the story of the New Jersey Forest Fire Service and the story of 100 years of firewardens and firefighting equipment battling wildfires in order to protect lives, property, and New Jersey's natural resources. This 1949 photograph captures section forest firewarden William Hagerthy and a firefighter testing the fire pump on a Dodge WM Power Wagon off-road engine in the New Jersey Pine Barrens. If this moment was returned to 1906 or advanced to 2006, the two significant elements would still be present, firewardens and firefighting equipment. Through photographs and their descriptions, this book will tell the story of the forest fire service, from its beginning in 1906 to reaching a major milestone of providing 100 years of public service and public safety to the state of New Jersey, while showing the transformation of the firewarden system and firefighting equipment over this last century.

The New Jersey Forest Fire Service was established by law on April 18, 1906, (Chapter 123, Laws of 1906) and the act became effective on July 4, 1906. During this century, tremendous progress has been achieved in the battle against untamed wildfire, and many firsts have occurred in this state in the pursuit of controlling it. New Jersey was an early pioneer in the use of aircraft in forest fire control operations. The forest fire service was instrumental in the research, design, and development of off-road engines to provide a quick initial attack engine that has played a significant role in reducing the size of most wildfires and minimizing losses to life and property. The state is a nationally recognized leader in fire management and the use of prescribed fire. Prescribed fire use can be traced back to the early years of the forest fire service on both public and private lands. The forest fire service has shared this knowledge along the way and has assisted the wildland fire management community on a local, regional, and national level. Over the years, various agencies have come to New Jersey to study forest fire service programs and have patterned their operations after New Jersey's. Local fire companies have been assisted by training provided by firewardens as well as equipment and funding through the Federal Excess Personal Property and volunteer fire assistance programs. The forest fire service has also provided their expertise and assistance to other states and federal agencies since 1985 through a national cooperative forest fire protection agreement. The history of the forest fire service is one that reflects both the development of forestry and forest fire control programs in America.

This book has been divided into six chapters, which include early years, lookout towers, vehicles and equipment, firewardens and firefighters, wildfire views, and fire cache. Each chapter will highlight many of the firsts as well as many of the significant happenings and achievements gained by the New Jersey Forest Fire Service in these 100 years. New Jersey's topography is very diverse, ranging from rugged hilly terrain at High Point on the Kittatinny Ridge, south through the sandy and remote pine barrens, and ending at Cape May's beaches, and this book has captured these differences and how they influenced the evolution of the forest fire service to meet these challenges from a fire protection standpoint.

The early years looks at the years between 1906 and the 1940s, and relates how forest fire protection responsibilities were first outlined in New Jersey and how they set the framework for the growth and expansion of the forest fire service. During this time period, the forest fire service evolved from a system that used local firewardens with minimal equipment to a statewide organization beginning to acquire the most modern equipment and technology to meet its goals. Lookout towers describes the importance of the basic system of fire detection and how it evolved to become a statewide system that is responsible for reporting over half of the wildfires that occur in New Jersey as well as initiating a quick and organized response of firefighting resources.

Vehicles and equipment have always been a cornerstone of the forest fire service's fire protection program in providing an organized and equipped attack on all wildfires. Vehicles have evolved from basic capabilities and designs to utilizing the most modern types to design and construct a fleet of off-road wildland engines that are capable of utilizing quick and effective direct attack methods in order to keep wildfires small and losses minimal. For many years, the Dodge Power Wagon was the backbone of the forest fire service's fleet, and their changes and development over the years will be highlighted. Firewardens and firefighters looks at the changes and developments in New Jersey's firewarden system over the years. Many photographic moments have been preserved of the day-to-day as well as firefighting duties of full- and part-time employees of the New Jersey Forest Fire Service. This chapter also looks at some of the leaders and key personnel in the organization over the last 100 years. Aviation and fire discusses the development of the forest fire service's aviation program from 1927 to the present and looks at the proactive use of aircraft for aerial detection, fire suppression, and the aerial overview and command and control of wildfires. Over these years, New Jersey has utilized a mix of fixed wing and rotary wing aircraft provided through private contractors, state purchase, and the loan of federal aviation resources.

Wildfire views presents a chronological look at wildfire activity across New Jersey and briefly describes a sampling of serious wildfires that have caused great losses and devastation to people and improved property, as well as New Jersey's rich natural resources. Large devastating wildfires have occurred during periods of dryness and drought and may occur during any month of the year. Each year, New Jersey experiences an average of 1,600 wildfires, and many photographic images of firefighters battling these fires have been preserved in this chapter. Fire cache provides a place for photographs from a mix of forest fire service programs and activities that have been very successful and have assisted in promoting a positive image of the forest fire service as a key public safety agency within the state of New Jersey.

The images in this book have captured a sample of moments in the 100-year history of the New Jersey Forest Fire Service and will help celebrate the valuable service provided to New Jersey, as well as preserving these memories for all to enjoy.

—Maris G. Gabliks, State Firewarden

One

THE EARLY YEARS

Wildfire has been a major factor in New Jersey's environment since prehistoric times. Natural fires and Native American burning played a major role in shaping the land and providing the vast expanses of forestland that greeted early settlers. Pioneers adapted the Native American practice of burning the woods to clear land for agriculture. An early account of a fire in 1755 reported a 30-mile-long fire front between Barnegat and Little Egg Harbor. However, very little was done to control wildfires in New Jersey before 1900. Reports of the state geologist indicate that during the late 1800s, it was common for 70,000 to 100,000 acres to burn annually in the pine barrens region of the state. Individual wildfires of 20,000 acres or more were not unusual.

In 1899, Gifford Pinchot, working as a consultant to the state geologist, submitted a report emphasizing the need to control wildfires in New Jersey, and without forest fire protection, forests could not be managed for public benefit. As a result of this study, the Forest, Park and Reservation Commission was established and the first forest protection laws were created. As a follow-up to increasing forest fire protection measures, the New Jersey legislature enacted a law establishing the forest fire service in 1906. The law took effect on July 4, 1906, and the New Jersey Forest Fire Service was born. At this point, the forest fire service consisted of a state firewarden and his initial job was to approve the appointment of township firewardens for each municipality in the state that was forested. The township firewarden was the local representative in charge of the forest fire service for that jurisdiction. A total of 73 township firewardens were appointed that year, and shovels were purchased for issue to firewardens for fighting fires.

Soon after, the forest fire service was subdivided into four geographical divisions with a division firewarden in charge of each. In 1924, the forest fire service was restructured from a local system to a state centralized system with the abolishment of township firewardens and creation of tactical administrative areas with a section firewarden in charge. This change set the stage for the modern forest fire service organization that exists today.

This December 29, 1908, photograph shows one of New Jersey's first forest fire lookout towers used to quickly detect wildfires. This tripod-style fire tower was 30 feet tall and was constructed for a total cost of $10. This tower was located in Woodmansie, Burlington County, in the pine barrens region of New Jersey.

This backfire was ignited along this narrow road in order to hold a threatening wildfire from jumping the road near Pasadena on May 13, 1908. At this time, the forest park reservation commission believed that forestry was impractical in New Jersey until wildfires that burned each year could be brought under control. From November 1, 1908, to October 31, 1909, some 563 fires burned over 93,225 acres, with losses to forests and improved property totaling $133,944. A total of $13,772 was allocated to the forest fire service that year for its expenditures.

During the early 1900s, railroads were responsible for causing a great number of wildfires across New Jersey. State forest fire laws required that railroads maintain firebreaks with fire lines on each side of the tracks to prevent wildfires from spreading beyond these cleared buffer areas. This photograph depicts this requirement on the Pennsylvania Railroad line east of the Browns Mills Junction on February 8, 1910.

During 1910, the forest fire service established three new lookout towers to assist with the quick detection of wildfires and rapid response of men and equipment to these fires. Towers were constructed at Batsto, Four Mile, and Dukes Bridge. The Four Mile tower was of a simple tripod construction and located in central Burlington County.

In 1910, the Wharton and Northern Railroad was not required to construct railroad fire lines along its rail lines due to an agreement with the forest fire service. The railroad agreed that protection of the forests would be provided by means of a high-speed motorcar, equipped with a water tank and firefighting tools, which would run behind each train whenever the forests were dry and capable of being burned.

This fire line, constructed in 1908 on the Bass River Forest Reserve, consisted of a totally cleared road and 40 additional feet on the right cleared of all brush with only the best trees remaining. The creation of fire lines was critical to keep fires out of the early forest reserves. A fire line consisting of only a road width totally cleared to mineral soil could be constructed for $4 per mile.

This 1911 photograph shows Victor Bush of Pemberton Township alongside his firefighting wagon. During his tenure with the forest fire service, Victor Bush served as a township firewarden (appointed by the township committee and approved by the state firewarden), district firewarden (appointed by a township firewarden to cover part of their territory), and a forest reserve warden for Lebanon Forest (appointed by the Department of Conservation and Development).

This 1914 photograph shows an area of pine forest near Magnolia (Burlington County) burned repeatedly to protect adjacent cranberry bogs from the potential damage of a devastating wildfire. Cranberry growing was a leading industry in south Jersey during this time period. The use of fire to protect cranberry bogs is one of the first documented uses of prescribed fire in New Jersey as a fire management and public safety tool.

FOREST FIRES

BURNING BRUSH or SETTING FIRE in or near the woods IS UNLAWFUL throughout the year in this township WITHOUT A WRITTEN PERMIT from the local Firewarden. Penalty for violation, $50 to $200.
A permit is not necessary if the fire is at least 200 feet from woodland or growth that may carry fire to the woods. Any legal FIRE MUST BE WATCHED UNTIL it is ENTIRELY OUT. Penalty for failure, $50 to $200.

To cause A FOREST FIRE IS A VIOLATION OF THE LAW. Penalty, $50 to $200.
A Firewarden's permit gives no release. Ignorance of the law is no excuse. Poor judgment or mishap relieves no one.
SMOKERS are warned that dropping lighted matches or tobacco in or near the woods may render them liable to this fine and do unguessed damage as well.

FIREWARDENS CAN ARREST ANYONE FOUND VIOLATING THE LAW

Small fires may grow larger and do your neighborhood much harm. Each fire stopped when small means increased property value to you and your neighbors. Put out at once any that you find, or, if you cannot do so, summon help.
All such fire-fighters are paid for their work if the local Firewarden is told of and approves the service within ten days after the fire.

John Jones Firewarden
Centre Township
BY ORDER OF THE FOREST PARK RESERVATION COMMISSION OF NEW JERSEY, STATE HOUSE, TRENTON.

This new fire poster was issued in 1913 by the forest park reservation commission and was to be posted in any area of the state where the forest fire law was in effect. The forest fire service recognized the fact that the ultimate control of forest fires depended upon personal care in handling fire, so a special effort was made to reach the public, which was responsible for causing the fires.

Larry Terhune, 20 years old at the time, at Nolan's Point (near the shore of Lake Hopatcong) was compensated $60 a month for himself and his horse plus 10¢ per hour for fighting forest fires in 1914 as part of a fire patrol that was funded through the Federal Weeks Law.

14

This 1919 photograph shows a fire crew fighting a wildfire near Magnolia with shovels and backpack fire pumps. Due to the lack of available manpower during this time period, the 1920 state legislature increased rates of pay for firewardens and helpers. Rates were increased to $2 for two hours or less and 50¢ per hour thereafter for wardens, and $1 for two hours and 50¢ thereafter for helpers. (Photograph by Oscar Applegate.)

This photograph appeared in the 1920 annual report of the state firewarden, C. P. Wilber, and shows a fire crew sanding out a forest fire. Sanding basically involved firefighters using shovels to spray sand on the slower-burning portions of wildfires to extinguish them. This form of firefighting was most popular during this time period unless a water source was available close by.

This 1914 map shows which New Jersey townships were provided with fire protection coverage and had township firewardens appointed. All townships with the "W" symbol were provided with forest fire protection. The map also differentiates each township by percentage of forest cover into three categories: less than 25 percent, 25 to 50 percent, and more than 50 percent of the township covered by forest. In 1914, the forest fire service consisted of a state firewarden with an office at the state house; four division firewardens with offices in Dover, Lakehurst, Hammonton, and Millville; and 116 township firewardens.

16

As early as 1916, the forest fire service maintained a cooperative agreement with the Bell Telephone Company in which reports of forest fires transmitted to the telephone operator would be transferred to a firewarden who served as a point of contact for a given area. The image of this "Report Forest Fire to the Warden by Phone" metal sign was visible along roadsides throughout New Jersey.

This early fire prevention sign read, "A motorist dropped a lighted match here – result 2,000 acres like this – N.J. Forest Fire Service" and was placed along a roadside where a wildfire was accidentally ignited by a discarded cigarette. As early as the 1920s, the forest fire service promoted the prevention of wildfires. New Jersey's fire prevention problem was complicated by an intermingled mixture of densely populated areas and wilderness.

The pine plains forests that occur in the New Jersey Pine Barrens are considered globally significant, and the state's dwarf pitch pine plant communities are the largest in the world. The two largest sites in the pine barrens include the East Plains and the West Plains. Most scientists believe that the long history of frequent and severe wildfires has been responsible for the creation and management of this unique forest vegetation. This photograph was taken in June 1930, near Barnegat.

This 1930s photograph shows a local forest fire crew fighting a fire with a mix of brooms, shovels, and Indian tanks. In 1939, the forest fire service fleet of firefighting vehicles consisted of a total of nine units, and each was equipped with enough tools to support a fire crew of 25 firefighters. A great emphasis was placed on fire crews during this time period.

This June 19, 1930, photograph shows the devastation of a wildfire that burned through an Atlantic White Cedar swamp on Lebanon State Forest in May of the same year during a period of extremely dry weather. Damaged trees have already been harvested for use as forest products.

Some of the earliest prescribed burning conducted on New Jersey state-owned forests was for the creation of safety strips along roads. This March 2, 1937, photograph was taken at 5:50 p.m. along the northern boundary of the Lebanon Experimental Forest and shows a prescribed fire burning against the wind and being held on the edges of a 100-foot safety strip by the hand raking of a fire line in light underbrush.

This 1938 photograph shows the cross section of a Scarlet Oak tree that was cleared from a fire line being constructed by the U.S. Forest Service at the Lebanon State Experimental Forest in New Lisbon. Note fire scars from past wildfires in 1878, 1884, 1886, 1894, 1900, and 1902.

After their creation in 1933, the Civilian Conservation Corps (CCC) provided men and equipment to the forest fire service through a cooperative agreement for forest fire suppression work. This June 1935 photograph shows one of the CCC crews assigned to Company Number 225, Camp Number S 55, located at Bass River Forest. As part of their normal duties on Bass River Forest, CCC crews were instrumental in reducing fire hazards and constructing truck trails.

This *c.* 1935 photograph shows Forester Horace Somes Sr. in the center of two other individuals from the Bass River Forest CCC camp sitting on the running board of a truck. CCC personnel assigned to assist the forest fire service in fighting wildfires were placed in crews consisting of a foreman, two squad leaders, and 14 men. Crew assignments were distributed as spray men, water men, shovel men, broom men, and axe men.

A bulldozer assigned to the CCC helps build a road through the Bass River State Forest in the mid-1930s. This equipment was also available for fighting wildfires when requested by the forest fire service. Several CCC companies were active across New Jersey during the 1930s, stationed at places such as state parks, forests, and state-owned lands.

Firewarden Peter Crozer demonstrates the use of an adjustable fire nozzle. Field testing of a mobile pumping unit at Penn Forest in 1938 included a test that allowed a stream of water at the rate of 11 gallons a minute through a quarter-inch nozzle at the end of 10,000 feet of one-and-one-half-inch standard hose to maintain 35 pounds of pressure at the nozzle and 300 pounds at the pump.

Section firewarden Walter S. Wheeler stands beside his personal vehicle, which was adapted for firefighting duties, in Barnegat around 1944. Note the license plate that identified the operator of the vehicle as a section firewarden with the New Jersey Forest Fire Service. Wheeler also served as a local municipal judge. (Photograph by C. B. Cranmer.)

Two

LOOKOUT TOWERS

The Native Americans, who once lived in the land that became New Jersey, took advantage of natural topographic features to be on the lookout for wildfires that could threaten their villages. As early settlers came to New Jersey, they also experienced the power of wildfires, and thus kept a lookout for fires using natural features such as hills or climbing tall trees. As early as 1840, the cupola of the Batsto Mansion in Burlington County was used to keep watch for wildfires that may threaten the community. Another unofficial lookout included an area on Cedar Mountain in Western Passaic County that was also used for the same purpose. In the early 1900s, simple pole lookouts were constructed with local materials that were climbed by fire patrols during their normal rounds to improve the quick detection and location of fires. Rural U.S. Post Office mail carriers were even responsible for assisting with the fire patrol and fire lookout responsibilities.

The first officially sanctioned forest fire service lookout tower was McKeetown Tower in Atlantic County; it was constructed out of wood in 1917. During the 1920s and even into the 1940s, steel lookout towers were constructed throughout New Jersey by the forest fire service supplemented with federal funding through the Weeks Law and Clarke McNary Act. Over the years, private landowners and other forms of government in New Jersey have supplemented the forest fire service's system of lookout towers by constructing their own lookout towers to protect their property from wildfire. Since 1906, there have been over 50 separate sites and lookout towers utilized for the quick and accurate detection of wildfires.

Today the forest fire service operates a fire detection system of 21 lookout towers strategically located across New Jersey to provide for the quick detection of all wildfires and the quick and organized dispatch of firefighting resources to these reported wildfires. These lookout towers report half of all wildfires that occur in New Jersey each year. Lookout towers also have spotted wildfires in the adjoining states of Pennsylvania and New York and have assisted them on a routine basis.

THIS TOWER is one of the "Eyes of the New Jersey Forest Fire Service," which is ever on the alert to protect the forest for your enjoyment and use, and for the necessities and pleasure of future generations.

The New Jersey Forest Fire Service needs your co-operation and support.

Carelessness and indifference mean large fire damages.

LET'S STOP IT!

During the 1920s and 1930s, the forest fire service developed a series of lookout tower postcards that were made available to the general public for personal use and as a way of increasing public awareness of its important mission as well as increasing awareness of the danger of wildfires throughout New Jersey. The front of the postcard featured different towers. This card highlighted Retreat tower, which was located on Retreat–Sooy Place Road about one and a half miles southeast of Retreat. Retreat tower was relocated to Apple Pie Hill in 1950.

The back of each postcard featured a cartoon of the forest fire lookout tower and referred to the towers as Anti Forest Fire Demons. The cartoon described the duties of the forest fire lookout observers during the course of their daily normal routine.

24

Norman Rogers, lookout watchman of Cedar Bridge Fire Tower, looks out his window for signs of smoke in this 1925 photograph. In 1925, the forest fire lookout network consisted of 19 towers statewide. Towers were routinely manned from March through December and were considered an integral part in the quick notification and response of the local forest firewarden and crew. An estimate that year stated that New Jersey's forests were protected from wildfire by the forest fire service for a cost of 3.5¢ per acre.

Forest fire observer Kevin Drake sights in a wildfire by use of an alidade in the Milton lookout tower during May 1987. The alidade was first developed by firefighters in the early 1900s as a sighting device to determine the horizontal bearing of a fire from a lookout and then relay this information to firefighters on the ground. Two or more towers are needed to triangulate the specific location of a fire.

This wooden structure was the Normanook Lookout Tower, which was near where the present Culvers Lookout Tower is located today on the Stokes State Forest in Sussex County. This tower was built around 1910. The poles used for the construction of this tower came from the nearby forest. By 1918, a steel tower replaced this wooden structure.

In 1920, the forest fire service constructed this wooden lookout with a large box-like lookout cab. The tower was built on Bear Swamp Hill on the Penn State Forest in Burlington County around 1914. This lookout was destroyed by wildfire. The lookout was rebuilt but again was destroyed by wildfire. During the 1950s, a platform tower was built at the lookout site to aid in the detection of wildfires. By 1962, a steel tower was moved to Bear Swamp Hill. In 1971, the steel tower was destroyed in a crash of a U.S. Air Force jet.

In 1916, this wooden lookout was built near Cedar Pond on the Newark Watershed in West Milford. This 1928 photograph shows the ground level, where the quarters of the observer who worked in the lookout would stay. In 1932, this tower burned down due to a fire. In 1933, a new 68-foot-tall steel tower was constructed.

A wooden lookout tower was erected sometime after 1927 at the French Farm Headquarters at Bass River State Forest in Burlington County. It was believed that the ranger that lived and worked at the headquarters building would use the lookout to detect wildfires on the forest. In 1937, an 80-foot-tall steel tower was erected in cooperation with the CCC and is currently an active lookout tower.

This stone structure was the Kinney Tower in Kinnelon, Morris County. In 1919, the forest fire service manned the tower under an agreement with the Kinney Family, which owned a 5,000-acre estate on which the tower was located. Due to its location on private property, this lookout tower was not open to the public. This tower was also known as the Kinnelon Tower and was utilized by the forest fire service through 1943.

The Edison tower was erected in 1920 in Ogdensburg, Sussex County. The 50-foot-tall tower was built in cooperation with the New Jersey Zinc Mine Company, which was owned by the Edison Company, hence Edison Tower. The elevation of the tower site was 1,400 feet. When the property was sold, the tower was taken down and moved to Union Hill in Denville, Morris County, and later became known as Greystone Tower.

This is the first Blue Anchor Lookout Tower, which was a 50-foot-tall tower built by the forest fire service in 1921. Blue Anchor lookout stands near the Old Blue Anchor Inn, which was an inn during time of the Revolutionary War in what is now Winslow Township, Camden County. In 1933, this tower was replaced by a new 86-foot-tall tower that is in service today, the 50-foot-tall tower was moved to Stokes State Forest and is the current Culvers Lookout Tower.

In 1922, the forest fire service signed an agreement for the construction of a fire lookout tower on the property of the Browing Land Company. This 60-foot-tall steel tower is still in service on top of the Kittatinny Ridge about nine miles north of the Delaware Water Gap. Catfish Lookout Tower is currently within the boundaries of the Delaware Water Gap National Recreation Area.

The first McKeetown Tower was erected in 1917 on the Atlantic City Water Department property in Egg Harbor Township (Atlantic County).The tower was totally constructed of wood, and this type of tower replaced the earlier pole-type towers. This tower was the first officially sanctioned fire lookout tower in New Jersey by the forest fire service. The tower was knocked down in 1936, awaiting its replacement by a modern steel tower.

By 1936, a steel 80-foot tower replaced the older wooden tower at McKeetown. The photograph to the right captures a tower construction crew taking a break after constructing the tower to a height of about 40 feet. After the Atlantic City racetrack was built, the view from the tower was blocked, and in 1946, a proposal was put forth to build a new lookout tower on top of the new grandstand at the race track. This proposal was denied, and 20 feet of height was added to the existing tower to reach a total height of 100 feet.

In 1922, the forest fire service and the U.S. Navy entered into an agreement to place a lookout tower on top of the 200-foot-tall Airship Hanger at the Lakehurst Naval Air Station. This tower operated until World War II. After the war, it was used briefly but was replaced by the nearby Lakewood Tower in Ocean County. By 1949, the Lakehurst lookout was no longer in use but is still present on top of the airship hangar.

In 1964, the Mizpah Tower was moved from Route 40 and Estelle Avenue to Route 40 and Madison Avenue in Hamilton Township, Atlantic County. This photograph captures the tower being moved by crane. Over the years, several towers have had to be relocated either due to a loss of the view or by termination or changes in land-use agreements.

Batsto Lookout Tower was constructed as a 60-foot steel tower in 1924 near the site of the historic Batsto Village, which today is part of Wharton State Forest. Later a 40-foot section was added to the tower to reach a new height of 100 feet. This tower replaced the cupola of the historic Batsto Mansion, which has sometimes been referred to as one of the oldest lookout towers in the United States.

This 60-foot-tall tower was originally located on Chestnut Hill in the Old Bridge Village of East Brunswick. In 1963, the former Old Bridge Tower was moved to Thompson County Park in Monroe Township, Middlesex County, near Jamesburg. It is still in service as the Jamesburg Lookout Tower. The lookout tower was moved for a cost of $5,805 in 1963. (Photograph by John H. Rieth.)

Cedar Bridge Lookout Tower was first located at Cedar Bridge in Barnegat Township. In approximately 1935, the lookout tower was planned to be moved to Coyle Field along Route 72 in Woodland Township (Burlington County). A steel tower was constructed there to a total height of 125 feet in 1936. The existing tower was moved to Bass River State Forest. This tower at Coyle Field would be New Jersey's tallest steel tower ever constructed.

In 1983, the Cedar Bridge Lookout Tower was moved via helicopter from the remote area of Aserdaten, in Lacey Township, to a spot along County Route 539 in Lacey Township. Constant vandalism to the tower forced the forest fire service to move the tower in order to better protect it. This new location along Route 539 is the fourth location of Cedar Bridge Tower.

Three

VEHICLES AND EQUIPMENT

Early firefighting equipment utilized by the forest fire service included horses and wagons, shovels, buckets, and pine boughs. By the 1930s, the forest fire service initiated the purchase of trucks and vehicles to assist in the annual battle against wildfires. Early equipment included backpack pumps, backfire torches, portable pumps, and fire hose. Some of the first vehicles purchased were rack-body-type trucks that could be used to haul firefighting equipment and firefighters. Some rack-body trucks were fitted with tanks and cans to carry water to the scene of a wildfire. In 1937, a report recommended that the forest fire service acquire fire engines to assist in accomplishing their firefighting duties in a safer and more effective manner, and in 1938, the first commercial fire engines were purchased. Three Ford fire engines were purchased, and one was assigned to each division. Around 1940, the forest fire service started constructing its own fire truck bodies and installing fire pumps, tanks, and other equipment on to commercially purchased vehicles.

After World War II, military surplus vehicles and equipment were made available to the forest fire service through various programs. Jeeps, dozers, and other equipment were acquired and converted for forest firefighting duties. In 1946, the first Dodge Power Wagons were purchased and over the next several decades would be developed and constructed into highly effective and efficient off-road wildland engines. The idea behind the off-road engine was to be able to maneuver the engine as close to the perimeter of a spreading wildfire in order to conduct a direct attack and quickly control the fire and minimize its spread.

In 1964, the forest fire service fleet consisted of 61 firefighting trucks, nine passenger cars, two 1,200-gallon-tank trucks, six pick-up trucks, one service truck, two 2,000-gallon trailers, two D4 bulldozers, 12 tractor and plow units, and 41 portable pumps. Today's firefighting fleet has far surpassed the 1964 statistics and includes over 468 vehicles and pieces of heavy equipment immediately available for response to wildfires across New Jersey as well as being backed by a support system consisting of state-of-the-art technology.

Shown in this c. 1935 photograph is a portable power pump being operated on the bank of a woodland stream. Power pumps were kept at strategic locations throughout the wooded areas of the state, ready for use at a moment's notice by a district firewarden and crew. These pumps delivered 15 gallons of water a minute through a mile of hose. Knapsack spray tanks were filled from the small hose being held by the warden at the right.

This 1934 Chevy rack-body truck was among the first state-owned vehicles assigned to the New Jersey Forest Fire Service. This vehicle was purchased without any equipment. At a later date, a water tank was added with fire pump and hose reel. This truck was assigned to the Hammonton area.

This 1937 Chevy was one of several that were put into operation with the New Jersey Forest Fire Service during 1937. Backpack hand pumps, hand tools, buckets, and other small equipment were carried on the truck. Later 55-gallon drums filled with water were added. During the 1940s, a front-mounted pump and a water tank were added to these units. Prior to these trucks being purchased, firewardens would have to use their own vehicles or make arrangements with local farms or businesses for the use of their vehicles in assisting with fighting wildfires.

This 1938 Ford fire engine was one of three new mobile firefighting units delivered to the forest fire service that year as a result of a 1937 study and report that recommended that motorized fire apparatus be provided to the forest fire service for combating wildfires. The three units were assigned to Butler, Whitings, and Millville. By using these pumper fire engines, water was able to supplant the old and dangerous practice of backfiring.

In 1939, a Ford cab over engine was purchased. Several historical pieces of information are visible in this photograph. First, 1939 was the first year that the Ford Motor Company produced a cab-over-style vehicle, and second, this unit was one of the first cab-over-engine-style fire engines to be used in New Jersey.

After the successful use of the three 1938 Ford fire engines, an additional order of Ford fire engines was placed. The 1939 Ford fire engine had a different fire engine body style than the 1938 trucks. A different fire truck manufacturer was believed to have built the bodies on the 1939 units. Note the metal buckets on the rear of the truck that were used to extinguish fires.

A forest firewarden mans the statewide radio at state headquarters in Trenton in February 1943. This early radio system allowed the state headquarters, three field division offices, lookout towers, observation plane, and motorized fire units to remain in constant communications. A topographic map of northern New Jersey is on the back wall as well as a list of unit radio call signs that were in service by the division on the top right wall.

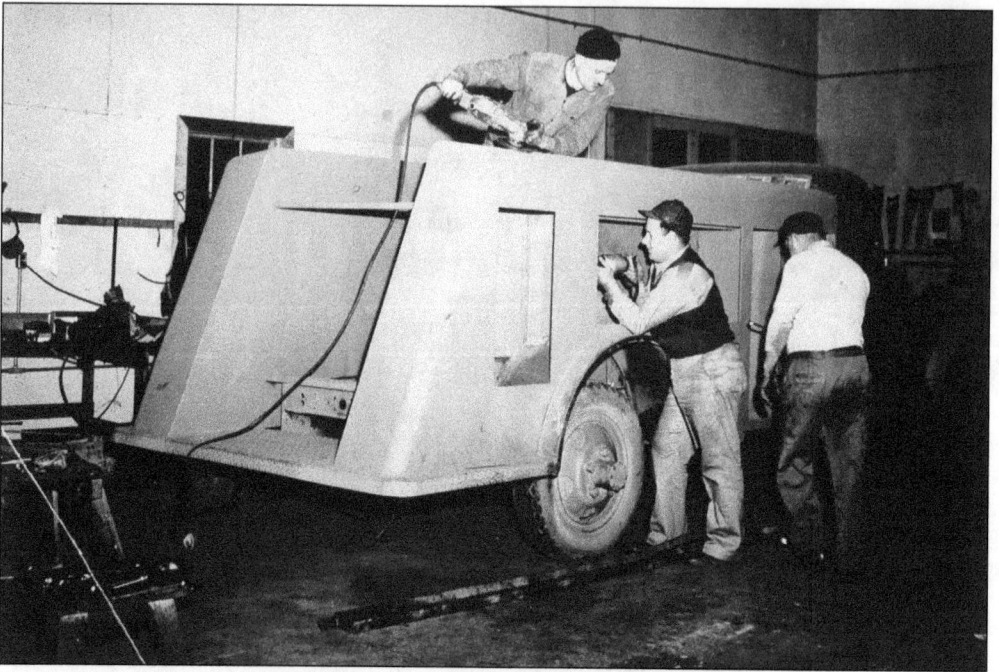

Besides having an airfield and hangar at the Trenton Airport in Baker's Basin, the forest fire service also operated its statewide shop from that facility. This photograph shows three forest fire service employees fabricating a fire truck body for the 1939 Dodge-style truck at the state shop. During this time period, the forest fire service employed a pilot, and part of his duties also included repairing aircraft as well as repairing fire engines and firefighting equipment.

This 1939 Dodge truck is believed to be outfitted with the first fire truck body built by New Jersey Forest Fire Service equipment personnel. The body was outfitted with a 500-gallon tank and a 250-gallon-per-minute fire pump. By constructing these fire engine bodies in house, the forest fire service was able to realize a cost savings over purchasing the bodies from a fire engine manufacturer.

40

During 1940, several Ford pick-up trucks were purchased by the forest fire service. Equipment maintenance personnel installed a two-way radio, a 250-gallon-per-minute front-mounted pump, and a 200-gallon water tank in the pick-up bed. The engine carried 500 feet of three-quarter-inch hose, 2,000 feet of one-and-a-half-inch hose, a portable pump, eight Indian-brand pumps, rich tools, brooms, axes, a first aid kit, and wrenches.

This c. 1940 view of the Baker's Basin Forest Fire Repair Shop shows two equipment specialists mounting a front-mount pump onto a 1940 Ford pick-up truck. This was the first repair shop utilized by the forest fire service. Currently there are three regional shops, a research and development shop, and two airport facilities. The regional shops are located in Andover (Sussex County), New Lisbon (Burlington County), and Mays Landing (Atlantic County).

During 1940, several General Motors Corporation cabs and chassis were purchased by the New Jersey Forest Fire Service. The bodies for these vehicles were also fabricated by forest fire service equipment personnel. These units had a 250-gallon-per-minute pump and a 500-gallon water tank. Compartments were fabricated into these bodies for carrying equipment and supplies. Note that the use of body compartments was not a common practice on any fire engine during this time period.

During 1946, a total of 10 Dodge WM Power Wagons were purchased by the forest fire service. Three trucks were fitted with three different types of pumps. The vehicle was purchased at a cost of $1,950, the pump cost $150, the hose cost $50, and all equipment was installed for a cost of $300. After testing, the other seven vehicles were fitted with pumps as well.

A 1948 Dodge WM Power Wagon is demonstrating its pump-and-roll capabilities. These were the first four-by-four trucks used for fire suppression in the Pine Barrens areas of central and southern New Jersey. These trucks had the ability to pump and roll and could maneuver off road to complete a direct attack on a wildfire. No previous forest fire service engine was designed or able to perform this critical mission.

This 1947 FWD HA two and a half model was outfitted with a former army decontaminator unit that was acquired from the War Assets Administration. The pump was a Farquhar high-pressure pump capable of delivering 800 pounds per square inch. The forest fire service paid $5,092.10 for the vehicle, $673 for the decontaminator unit, and forest fire service labor for installation added up to $50.

After World War II, the War Assets Administration made available thousands of former military vehicles to state and local government agencies for conversion into fire apparatus. The truck pictured here is a 1941 Dodge half-ton four-by-four WC 4. This style vehicle was the predecessor to the famous civilian-style Dodge Power Wagon.

This Jeep was purchased from the War Assets Administration shortly after World War II for $342.50. The Jeeps were very adaptable in north Jersey due to their ability to operate in narrow places and on steep grades. The unit's biggest limitation was the small amount of water it was capable of carrying. The forest fire service purchased the pump for $333.50, and the tank was constructed for $10 in materials and $45 for labor.

This Clarkaire tractor is fitted with a Stubby Middlebuster Fire Line Plow from the Michigan Forest Fire Program. This was an experimental plow developed by firefighters in Michigan and hooked up to a New Jersey tractor for field testing by the New Jersey Forest Fire Service. William Staib is at the control of the tractor in this late 1940s photograph.

Five military surplus dozers were obtained by the New Jersey Forest Fire Service in the late 1940s. In this photograph, the five USTrac dozers were just acquired and were not yet retrofitted with brush protection and additional armor to protect both the operator and the machine when operating in the forest environment. The fabrication of the brush protection was to be completed at the Baker's Basin shop.

In 1950, two tractors were purchased from the Oliver Tractor Company for $ 2,890.70. By 1950, the forest fire service had a total of 10 tractor and plow units in service. They consisted of two Oliver HG models, three Clarkaire models, and five USTrac models. A fire plow was developed by the Oliver Tractor Company, A. C. Anderson Company, and the forest fire service.

In 1951, a total of 12 FWD half-ton vehicles were purchased by the forest fire service. Eleven of the units had the same body that carried a small pump, a 500-gallon water tank, 500 feet of three-quarter-inch hose, a hose reel, six Smith backpack pumps, six fire brooms, six fire rakes, and 1,000 feet of one-and-a-half-inch hose, as well as a two-way radio. The 12th truck carried a high-pressure John Bean brand pump.

On November 8, 1951, this operator of a FWD brand fire engine demonstrates how this all-wheel-drive engine can maneuver through forest vegetation to directly attack a wildfire with the use of water. As the photograph was taken, the vehicle was in the process of knocking over small trees in the vehicle's path to reach a possible wildfire.

In 1952, an additional FWD four-by-four half-ton vehicle was purchased. This unit had a much different body than the order of vehicles received in 1951. This unit appears to have a much larger engine-driven pump. The FWD Company was started in 1912 by Otto Zachaw and his brother-in-law William Besserdich in Clintonville, Wisconsin. Later Besserdich left the company to found the Oshkosh truck company in 1917.

Throughout the 1950s and 1960s, several orders of Dodge WM 300 Power Wagons were received. By the 1950s, all units in the central and southern areas embraced the technique of running down fires by pushing over brush and smaller trees to reach the forest fire as fast as possible. Additional brush protection helped protect the trucks from operating in thick forest vegetation.

This 1962 Dodge WM 300 was in service until 1979. Engine C-19 had a 300-gallon water tank and was also capable of pulling a trailer in which an International 500 Tractor and Plow was transported. C-19 appeared in many firemen's parades throughout southern New Jersey and earned many trophies for outstanding appearance. (Photograph by H. J. Swartz.)

In the 1970s this 1953 M-54 five-ton six-by-six Federal Excess Property Truck was converted into wildland engine B 39. The unit was outfitted by the crew of Section B-7 in the Toms River area. The truck was fitted with two nozzles on the front of the truck, and an operator could control both nozzles from the elevated roof dome. (Photograph by Steve Holmes.).

After World War II, the New Jersey Forest Fire Service acquired vehicles and equipment from the federal government through various programs. Over the years, hundreds of vehicles have been acquired and converted for wildland and rural firefighting duties. Engine B-31, a late 1950s M-35 six-by-six military truck that was used as an off-road tanker to provide a water supply in inaccessible areas, was stationed at the Whiting Volunteer Fire Company.

During the 1960s, several Dodge W-500 chassis were purchased by the forest fire service. This style truck was the heaviest duty Dodge Power Wagon ever produced. At least four of these units were placed into service in central and southern New Jersey. Several of these units were outfitted with bodies that were reutilized from 1939 and 1940 vintage Dodge and GMC fire engines. One such unit was even fitted with a front spray-bar system.

District forest firewarden Bob Bethanis is driving B-20, a Dodge W-500 off-road engine, at an April 1981 wildfire in Little Egg Harbor Township (Ocean County). The firefighter in the well is district firewarden Larry Oliphant. This photograph appeared in a local newspaper the day after the fire, with a headline stating that these hot, dusty, and tired firefighters worked hard to control this forest fire.

In the later half of the 1960s, several International 500 tractor-plow units were purchased to replace some of the older units acquired in the 1940s and 1950s. The first International tractors were gasoline powered, and later units were ordered with diesel engines. (Photograph by H. J. Swartz.)

In 1970, Dodge W-300 four-by-four step-side pick-ups were purchased by the forest fire service for conversion into off-road engines. This style Dodge replaced the WM Power Wagon. These trucks were fitted with pumps, tanks, and a full brush cage by forest fire equipment personnel. This model engine carried a 200-gallon tank with pump, hose reel, and winch. This unit was assigned as unit C-11 in 1975. (Photograph by John Toomey.)

During the 1980s, the forest service converted a 1970 Consolidated Electric M-561 six-by-six Gamma Goat into an off-road engine. The vehicle was acquired from the military through the Federal Excess Personal Property Program. MU 94 is equipped with a 250-gallon-per-minute fire pump and a 300-gallon water tank and is currently in service in northern New Jersey. (Photograph by John H. Rieth.)

During the early 1970s, Dodge redesigned the W-300 Power Wagon with a more modern design. This rig is from the first order placed with Dodge with the new cab style. These first units came with a step-side pick-up body. At least six of these units were placed into service across New Jersey. Engine B-3 is pictured in this photograph and was a 1973 model. (Photograph by Ricky Haines.)

In the mid-1970s, four International one-ton four-by-four pick-ups were purchased to be utilized as off-road engines. Some were fitted with fire truck type bodies and some came with a step-side pick-up body. Engine B-10 is shown in this photograph and was assigned to the Middlesex County area. No other orders for the Internationals were ever placed. (Photograph by Ed Schoonmaker.)

This c. 1965 Kaiser M-35 six-by-six two-and-a-half-ton truck was converted into a water tender during the early 1980s. This unit was kept in Pine Hill in Camden County and operated by district warden Al O'Neill. C-29 had a 1,000-gallon water tank and a 250-gallon-per-minute pump. A riding position or "well" was at the rear cab. A firefighter, Dave Pluck, is seen riding in the well. By the early 1990s, this truck was taken out of service. (Photograph by Shirley O'Neill.)

This unit is a Bombardier tracked vehicle. This all-terrain unit can access steep and rocky, rugged areas as well as operate in wetland forests and marshes. Unit 105 is a 1976 Bombardier equipped with a fire pump and an 80-gallon water tank. Pictured are supervisor of equipment William Resch (left) and division firewarden Edward Schoonmaker. (Photograph by Edward Gandolfi.)

Division A personnel utilized Jeep vehicles from the 1940s through the 1990s. In 1970, several CJ7 Jeeps were purchased and fitted with small pumps and water tanks. This 1978 photograph shows A-8, a 1976 model Jeep, with operator Wes Powers. At the time of this photograph, Unit A-8 was stationed at Stokes State Forest is Sussex County.

This 1977 International Loadstar four-by-four chassis had a utility body mounted by forest fire service equipment specialists. This is an unusual-looking truck due to its short wheel base. It has a 250-gallon-per-minute pump and carries 500 gallons of water. This truck has been nicknamed the "Chicken Wagon" by its crew due to its unusual appearance.

In 1968, the first John Deere 350 tractor was acquired by the forest fire service. This tractor would be followed by over 25 additional John Deere 350 units from 1977 through 1986. Each unit, except for two stationed in northern New Jersey, came equipped with a Fesco brand fire line plow. Many of these units have been rebuilt over the years, and 25 are currently in service. The pictured unit is MU 213, a 1979 John Deere 350 tractor, which is assigned to the Ocean and Monmouth County area. (Photograph by John H. Rieth.)

Two John Deere 350 wide-track dozers were purchased in 1979 for assignment to central and southern New Jersey. These wide-track dozers are capable of spreading their weight out over the wider tracks, which allows these dozers to operate in much wetter areas, such as swamps and wetland forests. Both units have a small fire pump and two 150-gallon water tanks mounted on both sides of the machine. Unit MU 212 is a 1979 John Deere 350 assigned to central New Jersey. (Photograph by John Rieth.)

During the late 1970s, the forest fire service received additional Dodge Power Wagons. This is the first time utility service bodies were installed on the off-road Dodge vehicles. Additionally the vehicles were outfitted with a 250-gallon-per-minute pump, 300-gallon water tank, and brush cage and armor to complete the job. Engine A-7 is a 1979 year model and was photographed at Liberty State Park in Jersey City with the lower Manhattan skyline in the background. (Photograph by Willie Cirone.)

This large former military M-932 five-ton six-by-six was obtained from the Federal Excess Property Program and was converted from a truck tractor with a fifth wheel into a water tender by equipment personnel in Division C in the late 1990s. Water Tender C-24 operates in the Millville area. The chassis was built in 1984 by the American Motors Corporation, and this unit has a 250-gallon-per-minute pump and holds 1,200 gallons of water. (Photograph by John H. Rieth.)

Over the years, the forest fire service has operated an assortment of medium and large bulldozers. These units are used in constructing fire lines on large fires and making fire roads into inaccessible topography. Many of the larger dozers were obtained through the Federal Excess Personal Property Program. Transport 93 is a 1980 International Truck Tractor tractor with an Eager Beaver trailer, and MU 413 is a 1989 John Deere 750 Dozer. Other large dozers currently in service include a Cat D7, Fiat-Allis, and a Cat D6LPG. (Photograph by John H. Rieth.)

Throughout the 1980s several orders of Dodge Power Rams were received. The Power Ram replaced the Power Wagon in 1980. Several dozen of these units were placed into service throughout the 1980s. Engine B-35 is a 1986 outfitted with a 250-gallon-per-minute pump and a 250-gallon tank. In 2006, a total of 17 of the late 1980s vintage Dodges remain in service. (Photograph by John H. Rieth.)

During the early 2000s, a 1988 GMC Brigadier chassis was obtained and a new 2001 Warren Forestry Body was installed at the research and development shop. A 2001 John Deere 450H Tractor Plow unit MU 220 is hauled to fires throughout central New Jersey by this unit. Many southern state forest fire protection agencies use this style vehicle to carry their tractor-and-plow units. (Photograph by John H. Reith.)

In 1996, the forest fire service purchased nine Dodge trucks to be converted into off-road engines. These vehicles were the last Dodge trucks added to the fleet before switching to a Ford vehicle. These were the new generation of four-by-four one-ton vehicles that make up the Dodge 3500 series. Engine C-4 was one of the first to be placed into service by the forest fire service. These units had a utility body, a fire pump, and a 250-gallon water tank installed. (Photograph by John H. Rieth.)

Between 1999 and 2000, a total of 10 Ford F-350 four-by-four chassis were purchased for construction into off-road engines. These were the first Ford four-by-four vehicles ever used by the New Jersey Forest Fire Service for this purpose. A total of 14 such units were constructed at the forest fire service equipment research and development facility. Each unit has a 250-gallon-per-minute pump, a 250-gallon water tank, and a Ford Power Stroke Diesel Engine. Engine A-4 is pictured. (Photograph John H. Rieth.)

This tractor and plow is a 2001 John Deere 450H model. Two were purchased with their assignments to central and southern New Jersey. These units are much more powerful, capable, and maneuverable than the previous tractors operated in New Jersey. The tractor is capable of operating three different implements that include a winch, a Fesco brand fire line plow, or a Fesco brand forestry disc. (Photograph by John H. Rieth.)

In 2003, three General Motors Corporation Top-Kick vehicles were delivered to the forest fire service. These vehicles are equipped with Caterpillar Diesel engines. The photographed unit was constructed into a Type 3 Engine that is capable of having a tractor-and-plow unit on a tagalong trailer. Each unit has a 250-gallon-per-minute pump and a 750-gallon water tank. Engine B-15 routinely operates in the Toms River area. Additional GMC Top-Kick vehicles were purchased in 2005. (Photograph John H. Rieth.)

Four

FIREWARDENS AND FIREFIGHTERS

In 1906, the initial firefighting force of the New Jersey Forest Fire Service consisted of a state firewarden and a system of township firewardens that were responsible for overseeing the forest fire service in their local jurisdictions. These township firewardens were authorized to appoint district forest firewardens who assisted them in completing their fire protection duties and maintained crews of firefighters available for firefighting assignments. Shortly thereafter, the forest fire service was divided into regional areas called divisions, with a division forest firewarden in charge. At first, four divisions existed, but the number was reduced to three administrative divisions by 1916.

In 1924, the forest fire service was reorganized from the township firewarden system to a system of tactical operational units called sections. Each administrative section was overseen by a section forest firewarden. This change took several years to take effect, and some township firewardens were still appointed into the 1930s. In 1929, there were a total of 31 administrative sections statewide. The numbers of sections has changed over the years based on overall acreage covered and changes in fire protection responsibilities and demographics. Currently there are 29 sections statewide with a full-time section forest firewarden assigned to oversee fire protection and fire management responsibilities within their geographic area.

Over its first 100 years, the forest fire service has also relied on a highly trained and experienced workforce of part-time on-call firefighters. These part-time employees have worked in various capacities as district forest firewardens and deputies, special district firewardens, engine and equipment operators, and crew leaders, as well as firefighters and crewmen. These personnel have sacrificed much in their personal lives to devote their time and provide their expertise and service to the New Jersey Forest Fire Service.

Today the forest fire service consists of approximately 89 full-time permanent employees (ranging from forest firewardens, forest fire observers, and equipment specialists to customer service representatives, forest fire pilot, and airport manager), 269 district forest firewardens, and over 1,500 trained on-call wildland firefighters. Besides just providing their skills and knowledge to the state of New Jersey, these firewardens and firefighters are available for response anywhere in the United States based on wildfire mutual-aid requests.

This 1948 photograph was taken of the attendees at the third annual forest firewardens training school held at High Point State Park. High Point monument is clearly visible in the background of the photograph and is located at the site of the highest point in New Jersey. Several surrounding states are clearly visible from the vantage point offered by the Kittatinny Ridge at High Point monument.

10TH ANNUAL FIREWARDENS TRAINING SCHOOL
NEW JERSEY FOREST FIRE SERVICE
MADISON HOTEL   ATLANTIC CITY, N.J.
OCTOBER 12-14, 1955

This 1955 photograph shows the attendees at the 10th annual firewardens training school. During this session, discussion included organizing for large forest fires, equipment needs and replacement protocols, and supervision on large forest fires. Speakers covered firewarden cooperation with civil defense, the use of prescribed burning, planning and organizing, public relations, blow-up fire conditions, interstate compacts, U.S. Forest Service cooperation, and cooperation with the state police. (Photograph by Fred Hess and Son.)

Col. Leonidas Coyle served as New Jersey's third state firewarden. During his tenure, the system of township firewardens established in 1906 was converted into the system of tactical operational units called sections. In 1935, Coyle initiated the construction of a landing field, lookout tower, and fire equipment supply base. In 1938, this landing field was officially designated as Coyle Field by the Department of Conservation and Development.

This 1950s photograph captures, from left to right, Charles P. Wilber, Charles R. Erdman Jr., James Vessey, William J. Seidel, and Crosby A. Hoar. Charles P. Wilber was New Jersey's second state firewarden, serving from 1911 through 1923, and he later became state forester as well as the director of the Division of Forestry and Parks. William J. Seidel also served as the state's fifth state firewarden from 1945 to 1960.

Commissioner Charles R. Erdman of the state Department of Conservation and Economic Development examines the motor of one of 12 trucks being constructed for the forest fire service in December 1950. The new trucks were to be assigned to firewardens within the pine barrens region of southern New Jersey prior to spring fire season. From left to right are division firewarden Arthur Conover, Commissioner Erdman, and state firewarden William Seidel.

Capt. Leroy S. Fales served as New Jersey's fourth state firewarden. This 1939 photograph shows Fales at his office at forest fire service state headquarters in Trenton, receiving a report of fire conditions around the state from firewardens on the fire line by means of the ultra-high-frequency sending and receiving radio, which resembles a telephone receiver.

Section firewarden Virgil "Whitey" Francis drives engine B-7 as Bruce Sloan shoots a stream of water in this 1969 photograph. They are operating a WM Dodge Power Wagon off-road engine, which became the workhorse of the forest fire service during the 1950s, 1960s, and 1970s. The Power Wagon allowed firewardens in southern and central New Jersey the opportunity to encircle a wildfire with the engine in order to control fast spreading wildfires, which was not possible with earlier equipment and vehicles.

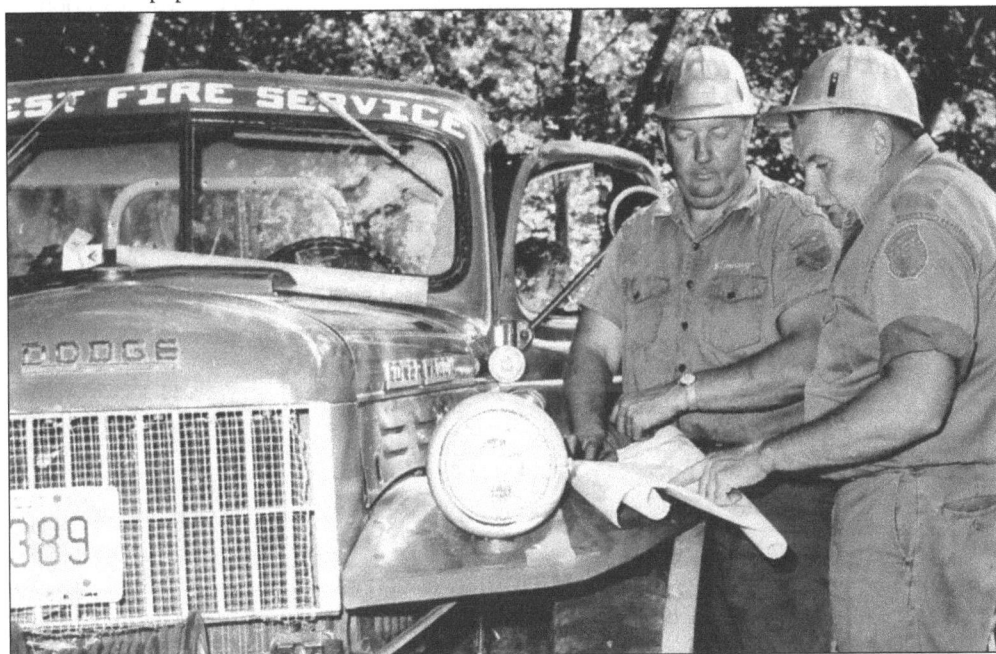

Section forest firewarden Eskil Danielson and district firewarden Bill Woltman discuss firefighting strategies over a map during a dry spell in September 1964. They are standing next to a WM Dodge Power Wagon off-road engine. The patch on their sleeves reads Department of Conservation and Development—New Jersey Forest Fire Service.

On January 16, 1947, a meeting was held for all section firewardens, division headquarters staff, and state headquarters staff. The following personnel, from left to right, attended from Division B (central New Jersey): (first row) George Sloan (section 9), Walter Wheeler (Section 4), Calvin Cutts (staff section firewarden), Bernard Bartlett (division firewarden), John Saturday (chief staff section firewarden), John Astbury (staff section firewarden), and Joseph Holloway (Section 2); (second row) George Bayer (Lakewood Station), Irwin Stackhouse (Section 5), Paul Linfoffer (Section 7), Charles Rogers (Cedar Bridge Station), Howard Emmons (Farmingdale Station), James MacDonald (Section 12), John Inman (Section 8), and Robert Lemmon (Section 6); (third row) Edward Tilley (mechanic), Paul Allen (Section 13), William Hagerthy ((Section 3), Carlton Taylor (Section 1), George Allen (Section 11), and George Etsch (Section 10).

The following personnel, from left to right, attended from Division A (northern New Jersey): (first row) Walter Lawrence (Section 9), Bert Callahan (staff section firewarden), Irwin Clement (division firewarden), Roy Meade (staff section firewarden), Ray Search (staff section firewarden), Russel Zeek (Greystone Station), and Ralph Colfax (Windbeam Station); (second row) Linn Lewis (Section 3), Lawrence Dunn (Section 8), Charles Meredith (Section 2), George Hart (Section 4), John Fisher (Section 7), Theodore Holz (Section 6), Eskil Danielson (Section 5), Squire Headly (Milton Station), and Lawrence Terhune (Section 9).

On January 16, 1947, a meeting was held for all section firewardens, division headquarters staff, and state headquarters staff. The following personnel, from left to right, attended from state headquarters: (first row) division firewarden Peter Crozer, deputy state firewarden R. Wesley Davis, state firewarden William Seidel, division firewarden Arthur Conover, and division firewarden Mortimer Bonham; (second row) radio engineer Giles Giberson, unidentified, airport manager William Staib, and unidentified.

The personnel that attended from Division C (southern New Jersey) included the following: (first row) John Brna (Section 5), Charles Challmers (staff section firewarden), Maurice Aaron (division firewarden), Frank Kovar (chief staff section firewarden), William Phoenix (staff section firewarden), and Rollen Mason (Section 2); (second row) Julius Frame (McKeetown Station), Charles Hughes (Section 10), Thomas Gerdau (Section 12), William Spencer (Section 3), and John Thornborrow (Section 4); (third row) Austin Maggioncalda (mechanic), George Post (Section 1), Arthur Boerner (Section 6), and John Brown (Section 7).

District firewarden Ken Badger (seated in truck) discusses firefighting tactics with Alby Gun at the scene of a wildfire in Laureldale (Hamilton Township, Atlantic County) in May 1977. The truck is a WM model Dodge Power Wagon. This style vehicle represented the backbone of the forest fire service vehicle fleet during the 1960s and 1970s. In 1977, New Jersey experienced 2,315 wildfires that burned over 39,387 acres of forest and open spaces.

This photograph was taken on May 25, 1976, at the scene of a wildfire in the area of Mizpah, Atlantic County. Staff section firewarden Harry Davenport (left) and section firewarden Ben Petrini stop for a break after controlling the fire. Off-road engine C-5 (Dodge Power Wagon W 300 model) is behind them. During 1976, 2,516 fires burned over 13,726 acres of New Jersey's forests. (Photograph by H. J. Swartz.)

This October 1969 photograph was taken of the attendees at the annual section firewarden training school. The attendees are standing in front of the Skylands Manor at High Point State Park along the Kittatinny Ridge. Besides forest firewardens, the group also includes representatives of the U.S. Forest Service, National Park Service, and New Jersey Forest Management Section.

This photograph was taken at the annual section firewarden training school during the fall of 1979. The photograph includes (front row) J. Hughes, D. Harrison, E. Schoonmaker, G. Koeck, J. Cumming, G. Bamford, G. Allen, E. Gandolfi, C. Rieger, F. Scardo, W. Lowert, and C. Anderson; (second row) R. Haines, J. MacMaster, R. Holmes, D. Sloan, H. Stillwell, R. Bentz, A. Smith, R. Dove, P. Hockenberry, S. Kwasnieski, P. Faubell, S. Hughes, C. Owen, B. Petrini, and P. Gerber; (third row) T. Tansley, V. Francis, W. Earlin, J. Gowdy, A. Liepe, R. Burrows, J. Hall, A. Younger, L. Wildrick, W. Woltman, C. Holsworth, D. Edelman, and E. Lempicki.

Section forest Firewarden Horace Somes and forest fire observer Walter Jennings man a forest fire service educational display at the New Jersey State Fair on August 13, 1989, at the Garden State Racetrack in Cherry Hill. The display board in the background highlights historic photographs of New Jersey wildfires and firefighting equipment used to combat fires over the past century. (Photograph by Shirley O'Neill.)

On August 21, 1973, the New Jersey Forest Fire Service mobilized two fire crews, consisting of 42 firefighters, to assist in battling a series of over 100 wildfires in Montana and Idaho. Leadership for the two crews included crew boss Vincent Ely of Monroe Township, Middlesex County; crew boss Edward Smith of Marlboro Township, Monmouth County; and assistant crew boss Alexander Drogotta of Elmer, Salem County. (Photograph by Whitey Swartz.)

A crew of firefighters take a photograph opportunity while conducting a prescribed burn at Allamuchy State Park on March 17, 1983. From left to right are (first row) Gerald Hendershot, Lloyd Wildrick, Edward Paladini, and Edward Schoonmaker; (second row) Robert Dove, Dave Edelman, Durward Strowbridge, Charles Lami, James Mangine, Ronald Papp, Joseph Haussman, Alf Andreassen, and Michael D'Errico

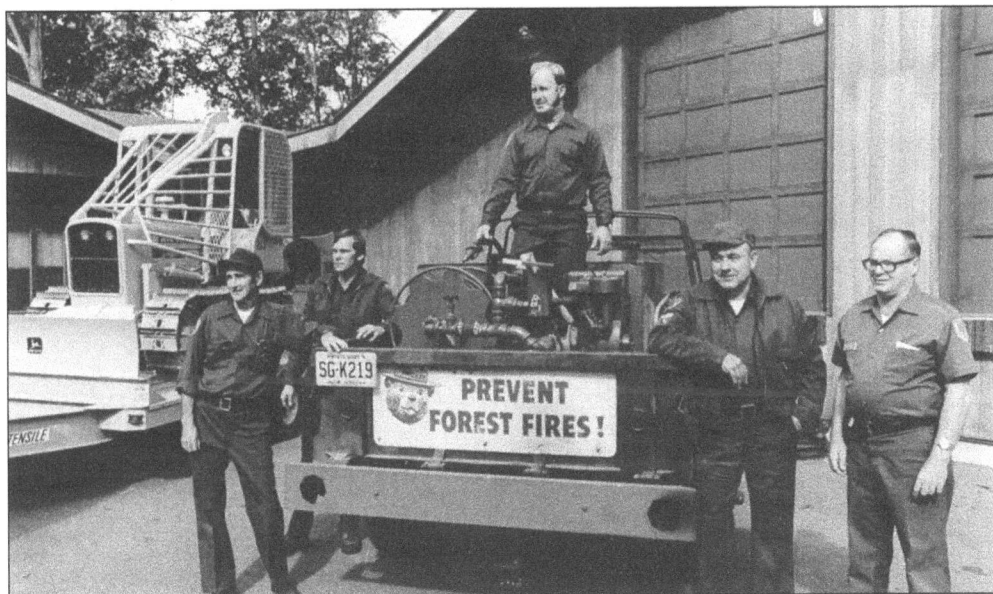

Section forest firewarden Albert Younger (far right) poses for this photograph with the fire crew at Allaire State Park in Wall Township, Monmouth County in October 1979. The Allaire fire crew consisted of Charles "Dusty" Rhodes, Tony Kopke, Peter Whitnum, and William Geshke. They are standing next to a Jeep pick-up truck, which was made available through the Federal Excess Personal Property Program and assigned to the park for conversion into an off-road wildland engine. A John Deere fire plow unit is in the left background.

William B. Phoenix served as New Jersey's seventh state firewarden. This early 1970s photograph shows Phoenix at his desk in the forest fire service state headquarters located in Trenton, along with his office assistant. Visible in the background is the Trenton War Memorial building and the dome of the state capitol on the state house complex, as well as the Delaware River, which separates New Jersey and Pennsylvania.

In 1980, division firewarden Paul H. Faubell received an award from the U.S. Forest Service for outstanding public service in forest fire prevention. Congratulating him are state firewarden James A. Cumming Jr. (left) and state forester Gordon T. Bamford. James A. Cumming Jr. served as New Jersey's eighth state firewarden from 1976 through 1982.

Staff section firewarden Horace P. Cook points out a wildfire location near Fort Dix to division firewarden Frank A. Kovar, who is transmitting this information via radio to a fire crew en route to the fire. This photograph was taken in June 1962 at the Division B administrative office in Pine Beach.

In 1988, the New Jersey Forest Fire Service received the DEP Excellence Award from the Department of Environmental Protection commissioner Richard T. Dewling for sustained performance in combating forest fires in New Jersey and the United States. From left to right are Thomas Miller, Carl Owen, Russel Fenton, Ray Holmes, Jeff Brower, Walter Earlin, state firewarden David B. Harrison, James Barresi, Kevin Drake, Commissioner Richard Dewling, James Gowdy, state forester Olin White, Edward Schoonmaker, and Steve Maurer.

State firewarden David B. Harrison addresses a crowd of attendees in front of the statehouse, as Gov. Thomas Kean listens to Harrison's remarks after receiving the "Jersey Pride" award for outstanding fire protection work by the forest fire service across New Jersey as well as the nation. Harrison served as New Jersey's ninth state firewarden from 1983 through 2001.

This October 1981 photograph shows a crew of firefighters, looking at a map, planning out prescribed burning fire lines in October 1981. Visible in the photograph, from left to right, are Butch Morris, Edward Gandolfi, Stanley Kwasnieski, Kenneth Badger Sr., and Jim McLaren. In the background is a tractor and plow awaiting use for the construction of fire lines.

Section forest firewarden Bill Lowery stands beside a forest fire service staff car with an Incident Command System (ICS) planning kit displayed on the trunk of the vehicle. This photograph was taken at a Mid Atlantic Interstate Forest Fire Protection Compact Meeting in Fort Indiantown Gap, Pennsylvania, during September 1974. The ICS kit was developed for quick deployment at expanding wildfire incidents so that the incident commander would have all necessary documents, forms, and paperwork in order to adequately document and manage the situation. (Photograph by Ed Schoonmaker.)

District firewarden Gary Crawford and fire crew members from Section A-1 take a break from constructing a fire line and discuss firefighting tactics during a live fire training session at the Ayers Farm on High Point State Park during an early spring day in the early 1970s.

Assistant division firewarden Jim Petrini (center) congratulates Jim Gowdy (left) and Jake Bruckner (right) on receiving Bronze Smokey Bear Awards for their service to the national Cooperative Forest Fire Prevention Program and outstanding work throughout the state of New Jersey spreading Smokey Bear's fire prevention message during Smokey Bear's 50th Birthday Celebration in 1994. This June 1995 photograph was taken in front of the Division C office in Mays Landing. (Photograph by Harold Swartz.)

District firewardens Al O'Neill and Steve White post a warning to drivers on Jackson Road in Atco that prescribed burning is being conducted in forest lands adjacent to the highway. Visible behind them is a tractor-plow unit that is utilized to construct and maintain fire lines that are necessary to facilitate prescribed burning operations. (Photograph by Shirley O'Neill.)

76

In 1988, the New Jersey Forest Fire Service was awarded the Jersey Pride award by Gov. Thomas Kean. State firewarden David B. Harrison accepted the award. Firefighters in the background assisted in combating wildfires in and around Yellowstone National Park that summer. Harrison is holding a bundle of tree seedlings that represent seedlings offered to the western states for reforestation projects.

New Jersey Crew No. 1 spent September 1–22, 1987, combating the Indian Wildfire on the Tahoe National Forest in Northern California. From left to right, firefighters include (sitting) Bob Wolff, Seton Herbert, Mike Drake, Carl Wendt, Louis Emmons Sr., Frank Zeller, Bert Plante, and Jim Garthaus; (standing) Gene White, Jim Mangine, Bill Orlandi, Tom Miller, Jim Barresi, Jeff Brower, John Earlin, Jim Dusha, Kevin Drake, Louis Emmons Jr., and Walt Earlin.

This photograph shows members of the state headquarters staff and Division C permanent personnel during the annual Division C district firewarden training meeting in 2000 at South Egg Harbor Fire Station. Pictured from left to right are (first row) Thomas Crim, Peter Bender Jr., Harry Fertig, Robert Gill, Larry Birch III, Edward Lord, and John Sanford; (second row) Glenn Liepe, Charles Hughes, Maris Gabliks, Edwin Jones, Vernon Stover, Russell Fenton, William Love, Steve Alcorn, Bob Amendt, Gary Burton, John Fowler, Mike Achey, Jeff Liepe, Frank Pallante, Henry Hasselhan, Bert Plante, Ken Badger, Steve Maurer, Ron Ruggeri, Dave Harrison, and Bill Donnelly.

The New Jersey Forest Fire Service provided several engine strike teams to the Texas Forest Service for wildfire deployments during the summer of 1998. This photograph was taken in front of a Texas Forest Service office with firefighters from the Texas Forest Service. New Jersey firefighters included Steve Holmes, Gene White, Bill Connellan, Donald Colarusso, Kevin Stout, and Glenn Shinn.

This c. 1950 photograph, taken near the scene of a fire in Section C-7 (Atlantic County area), shows firefighters and firewardens discussing firefighting operations. Included are Arnold Liepe, Henry Liepe, Harry Schabb, Herman Liepe Jr., Herman Liepe Sr., Donald Hand, and Brit Eaton. Note that the rear fender of the WM Dodge Power Wagon has been damaged from operating in the woods. (Photograph by Jack Boucher Jr.)

This photograph was taken of New Jersey Crew No.2 after flying into a remote spike camp by helicopter on the Huck Fire in Wyoming adjacent to Yellowstone National Park. Crew members included Walt Earlin, Jeff Brower, Russell Fenton, Mike Reed, Tom Gerber, Bob Meierjurgen, Maris Gabliks, Bill Edwards, George Gerber III, Steven Holmes, Dave Karpovage, Tom Sokol, Mike Strang, Louis Barthelemy, Robert Ellis, Alex Eristavi, Carl Wendt, David Misiuk, Bill Wilmouth, and Ronald Leach Jr.

This New Jersey Fire Crew helped fight the Corral Creek Fire on the Payette National Forest near Boise, Idaho, during the summer of 1994. Crew members included Jim Garthaus, Arthur Grimes, Chris Irick, Bob Meierjurgen, James Andrew, Edward Brook Jr., Stanley Brosko, Deale Carey, Brian Christopher, Robert Lemanski, Tim Nicol, James Parker, Mary Pat Povilaitis, Fred Schroeder, Frank Schoenstein, Bill Seeley, Glenn Shinn, Jay Weiner, and James Westura.

On June 22, 2002, Gov. James McGreevey hosted a reception at the Drumthwacket mansion in Princeton in honor of all firefighters who assisted in battling the Jakes Branch Wildfire in Berkeley Township on June 2 of that year. Pictured from left to right are section firewarden Thomas Gerber, state firewarden Maris Gabliks, section firewarden James Dusha, fire chief George Dohn, Governor McGreevey, unidentified, and Berkeley mayor Jason Varano.

New Jersey Fire Crew No. 1 was assigned to the Foothills Fire in Idaho in 1992. Crew members included Maris Gabliks, James Barresi, William Donnelly, Arthur Grimes, Dave Karpovage, Robert Meirjurgen, Jim Mangine, Russell Fenton, Bert Plante, Steven Holmes, Walter Leap Jr., Tom Sokol, Kenneth Metzler, Robert Gill, Steve Alcorn, Nels Warren, John Andreychak, Joe Root, and Christopher Irick. The New Jersey Forest Fire Service has provided wildland firefighters to 29 states since 1985.

A crew of firefighters pose for a photograph during a prescribed burning project on the Warren Grove Bombing Range in Ocean County during the 2005 burning season. The Warren Grove Bombing Range is located in the East Plains, which is an area comprised of dwarf pitch pine vegetation that is extremely flammable and a challenge to fire management personnel in implementing fire protection initiatives. From left to right are Ed Moniot, Rich MacMaster, Gary Welsh, Bert Plante, and Norman Welsh.

In 2005, the New Jersey Forest Fire Service initiated a pilot program called "Tracks" which utilizes blood hounds that are trained to track individuals that ignite wildfires. This photograph shows division firewarden Glenn Liepe introducing blood hound Blaze to a wildfire as well as the smoke that accompanies the fire. Blaze has also been a positive outreach and educational tool when visiting schoolchildren across southern New Jersey.

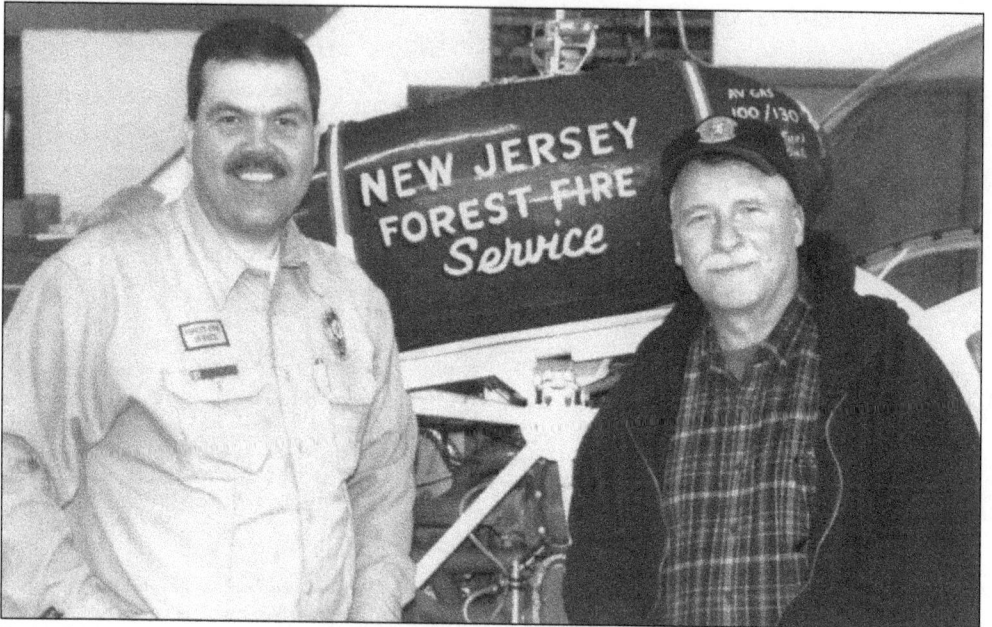

State firewarden Maris Gabliks (left) and supervisor of forest fire equipment Thomas Tolska stand in front of a forest fire service Bell 47 helicopter at Coyle Field in February 2006. Maris Gabliks became New Jersey's 10th state firewarden in 2001. The Bell 47 helicopter is a 1956 model and was acquired by the forest fire service through the Federal Excess Personal Property Program. It is primarily used for pilot training and aerial observation. (Photograph by Eric Tolska.)

Five

AVIATION AND FIRE

The use of aircraft has been an integral part of the New Jersey Forest Fire Service since 1927. Early aircraft were utilized for performing aerial observation of wildfires as well as relaying key information to forest firewardens commanding wildfire operations from the ground. Timely and accurate fire behavior observations and size-up information provided by the aerial observers and pilots assisted the firefighters in combating the wildfire as well as making wise and safe tactical decisions in controlling the fire. Colonel Leonidas Coyle was one of New Jersey's early state firewardens and pioneers who helped build the foundation for the aviation program of the forest fire service. Early aircraft utilized by the forest fire service included various types of fixed wing aircraft that were either leased or purchased by the State of New Jersey. With the development of rotary wing aircraft, the forest fire service proactively took advantage of this modern flight tool.

During the 1960s and 1970s, the forest fire service aggressively looked at aircraft and their important role in protecting lives, property, and natural resources from wildfire as a result of several significant wildfire seasons as well as the expanding and growing wildland/urban interface across the forested portions of New Jersey. During this era, the forest fire service studied and experimented with the use of helicopters and fixed wing aircraft. New Jersey was one of the early leaders in the nation in promoting the use of single-engine air tankers for a quick initial attack on fast spreading wildfires.

During the 1980s, single-engine air tankers provided by commercial operators were the primary fire suppression aircraft utilized in New Jersey, but by the late 1980s, state firewarden David B. Harrison was instrumental in reinstating a state-owned aviation program. This new program took advantage of acquiring federally owned helicopters through the Federal Excess Personal Property Program and making them available for aerial observation and command of wildfires on a year-round basis. Today the aviation program consists of a mix of state-owned fixed wing and rotary wing aircraft as well as a fleet of single-engine air tankers provided by Downstown Aero Crop Service, a New Jersey–based aviation contractor.

This contractor-provided Bell 47 helicopter was stationed at the Hopatcong Helistop in 1966. Pictured from left to right are Pete Swasey, Marshall Newman, Dane Roten, and Walt Jurman. This helicopter was equipped with floats so that it could float on a body of water and draft a load of water.

Division firewarden Stanley Hughes (center of photograph) stands with the helicopter pilot and helispot crew at Davis Field in Mays Landing during May 1970. The helicopter was a Bell 47 provided by a private contractor. Davis Field was named for state firewarden Wesley Davis after his retirement from the forest fire service.

This photograph was taken of New Jersey Crew No.6 in front of Helicopter 720, an Erichsen sky crane helicopter, at the Blackfoot Lake Wildfire Complex in Montana during the summer of 2003. The fire crew consisted of Deale Carey, William Cirone, Michael Achey Jr., Kenneth Barber, Ralph Wallen, John Holubowicz, Scott Wallis, David Achey, Patrick Mulvaney, Roger McLachlan, Kevin Eskow, Clint Travers, Todd Wyckoff, Michael Pretty, Burt Savage, William Maxwell, John Burkle, Robert Hills, Brian Christopher, and Scott Lidick. (Photograph by Willie Cirone.)

A pilot floats his Bell 47 helicopter on Lake Hopatcong in order to fill the helicopter's saddle tanks by way of a pick-up pump in April 1973. The helicopter is equipped with floats so it can pick up water from any lake and can quickly respond to a nearby wildfire, hover, and drop up to 90 gallons of water.

This Dromader single-engine air tanker is on contract to the forest fire service from the Downstown Aero Crop Service in Vineland, New Jersey. This aircraft is preparing for take off from Coyle Field in Burlington County for response to a reported wildfire. The Dromader can carry 600 gallons of water and foam with its aerial delivery on a fire consisting of either a salvo drop (all 600 gallons at once) or six individual drops of 100 gallons each.

State firewarden Leonidas Coyle surveys a South Jersey wildfire in an autogiro during a series of wildfires that burned over 28,000 acres in one day during the 1930 spring fire season. This aircraft was propelled forward by a conventional propeller but had the capability of sustaining the aircraft or allowing it to slowly and sharply descend through the use of horizontal revolving wings on a shaft above the fuselage.

A Bell 47 helicopter equipped with floats and saddle tanks hovers and drops water to demonstrate its effectiveness in making precision water drops on wildfires. This aircraft was utilized by the forest fire service during the 1970s and was also used to provide an aerial command platform for firewardens who were in charge of managing the fire.

R. Wesley Davis (left) and pilot Stanley Bowers look over a map and discuss a flight plan before setting off to conduct a reconnaissance mission of a wildfire. During the mid-1930s, the aircraft's priority was to fly the perimeter of a wildfire and allow an observer to draw the boundaries on a map and drop it to forest firewardens on the ground as well as communicating to them by radio. Davis later served as New Jersey's state firewarden from 1961 through 1968.

This Ag Cat biplane single-engine air tanker makes a drop on a wildfire during spring fire season in southern New Jersey. The biplane is capable of making one drop on a wildfire with up to 300 gallons of water. Class A Foam may also be added to the load of water to increase its effectiveness in knocking down a fast spreading wildfire. (Photograph by Shirley O'Neill.)

This 1969 photograph shows a Bell 47 helicopter dropping water from a fiberglass bucket. The helicopter provided an advantage over planes since it could hover over a fire and provide a precise water drop as well as being able to land near the fire scene, pick up a forest firewarden, and quickly provide them with an aerial overview of the entire fire scene and surrounding area.

In 1961, the forest fire service utilized a biwing Steerman aircraft for aerial bombardment of wildfires with water and retardant. This plane was stationed at Coyle Field, and this photograph shows a ground crewman fueling the plane while conversing with the pilot. During the 1961 fire season, this one aircraft delivered 5,220 gallons of retardant on wildfires across south Jersey.

Since 1982, the Ag Cat biplane has been the primary single engine air tanker (S.E.A.T.) utilized by New Jersey. The job of the S.E.A.T. is to arrive on any reported wildfire prior to ground forces and keep the fire in check until ground forces arrive. Since 1960, the average size of wildfires has been drastically reduced due to the combined quick initial attack of aircraft and ground resources on all wildfires. (Photograph by Tom Pogranicy.)

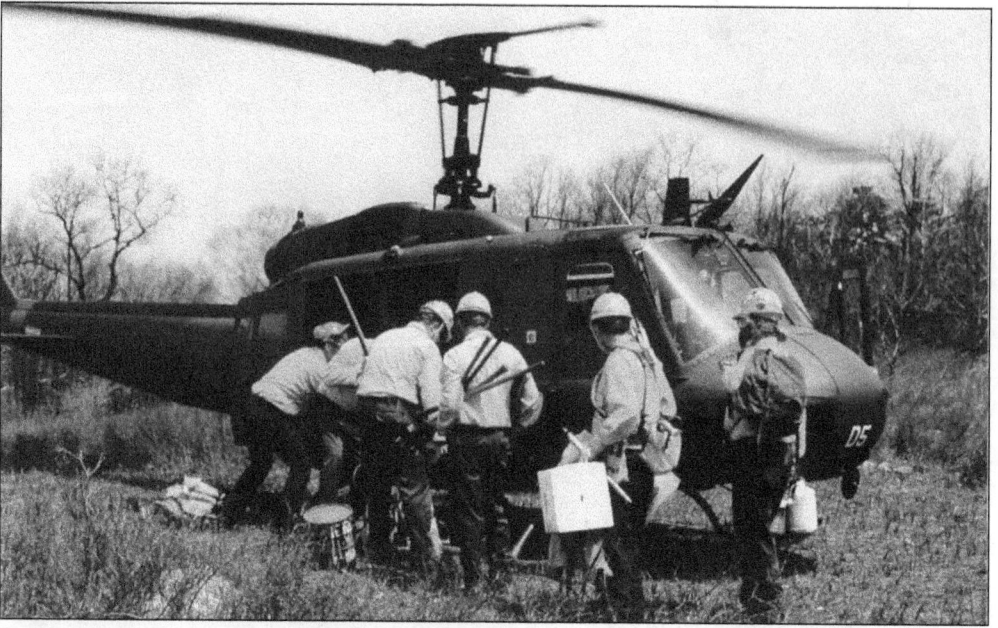

Besides dropping water on wildfires from a bucket, the Huey helicopter has been very useful in transporting firefighters to remote locations as well as transporting supplies and equipment. Helicopter Delta Five is seen picking up a crew of firefighters and their tools on a remote helispot on the Kittatinny Ridge near the Delaware Water Gap after completing the control of an 11-acre wildfire during the spring of 2000. (Photograph by Willie Cirone.)

This photograph shows the bird's-eye view that can be obtained by firewardens when they size up a wildfire from the air. This May 1967 photograph gives a view out of the bubble window of a Bell 47 helicopter and clearly shows a wildfire crowning through the tops of the pine barrens forest canopy. The Bell 47 helicopter was limited to only being able to carry the pilot and one observer.

In 1939, the forest fire service purchased this Beechcraft stagger wing swift cabin plane. The hangar in the background was located at Trenton Airport in Lawrence Township, Mercer County, along today's State Route 1 near Baker's Basin, which today is the site of the Quakerbridge Mall. The airport was owned by the forest fire service and operated as an airport and firefighting vehicle repair shop from 1940 through 1956.

On February 26, 1997, helicopter Delta 5 picks up a load of water with a bambi bucket under the control of forest fire pilot John Wimberg. This photograph was taken during a prescribed burning project in Salem County while the helicopter was picking up a 300-gallon load out of the Alloway Creek to support prescribed burning operations.

Section firewarden Frank Scardo and sea plane pilot Dave Quam look over a map and discuss a plan for aerial detection of wildfires in the Ramapo Mountain region. Their discussion took place on the shoreline of Greenwood Lakes in the late 1970s with Sea Plane Alpha in the foreground and off-road engine A-2 behind them.

In the late 1980s, the forest fire service reinstated its in house–operated aviation program through the acquisition of helicopters from the U.S. Forest Service through the Federal Excess Personal Property Program. The first three helicopters acquired included a Bell 47 and two Bell 206 Jet Rangers. These helicopters were primarily used for providing aerial observation and command to forest firewardens. In this photograph, helicopter Delta 3 carries a helitorch and dispenses a flammable gel to ignite a prescribed fire.

From left to right, Charles Full, William Naused, Edward Lord, Steven Holmes, and Louis Emmons Sr. stand next to a helitorch assembly at Colliers Mills Wildlife Management Area in Jackson Township, Ocean County, in the winter of 2001. Behind them is a Bell Jet Ranger helicopter that slings the helitorch for igniting fire for controlled applications. Visible smoke in the background is from a prescribed burning project that the helitorch was assisting with.

This Pitcairn mailwing aircraft was acquired by the forest fire service in 1930. At this point in the development of the forest fire service's aviation program, this fixed wing aircraft was primarily used for conducting reconnaissance on large fast spreading wildfires and relaying the fire behavior information to the firefighters on the ground. Aircraft were also a help in detecting newly started wildfires and expediting the response of firefighting resources to the fire.

Aeroflex-Andover Airport was acquired by the forest fire service in 1992 as a public general use aviation airport as well as serving as the primary air attack base for all firefighting aircraft in the northern region of the state. The airport's runways are surrounded by Gardener's Pond on the south and Lake Aeroflex on the north as well as being in the center of Kittatinny Valley State Park. It is often referred to as New Jersey's prettiest little airport. (Photograph by Ed Schoonmaker.)

A forest fire service Huey helicopter drops a load of water on the Rockwood II Wildfire, which started on July 29, 1997, in Hammonton, Camden County. The wildfire burned over 1,900 acres during a period of summer drought. The Huey helicopter can drop 300 gallons of water with a foam mixture to cool down hot spots and can quickly refill its bucket from a close by water source.

Six

WILDFIRE VIEWS

Every year, forest fire service firewardens and firefighters respond to over 1,600 wildfires across New Jersey. These wildfires damage forests and other natural resources, as well as threaten people's lives and improved property. Ninety nine percent of all wildfires in New Jersey are caused by people, either intentionally or accidentally.

The potential for wildfire disasters in New Jersey has been dramatically illustrated numerous times. Large conflagrations occurred several times from 1930 to 1992, and most recently in 1995. The most notable of the fires was on the weekend of April 20–22, 1963, when wildfires destroyed close to 190,000 acres of forest, consumed 186 homes and 197 buildings, and were responsible for seven deaths. In 1995, one wildfire burned 19, 225 acres in Ocean County, and during the summer drought of 1997, an 800-acre fire damaged 52 homes and threatened over 300 homes in Berkeley Township. The wildland urban interface is the term used to describe the placement of residential communities within forested areas. This trend is a problem not only across New Jersey, but nationally as well. Wildfires burning into developed areas have taken an increased toll on improved property. Several fires have reached disastrous proportions, destroying homes and taking lives.

The year 1930 holds the record for the most devastation in New Jersey as a result of wildfires. That year, 1,620 wildfires burned over 267,547 acres with an average fire size of 165.2 acres. One fire in 1930 burned over 49,000 acres and more than 100 buildings. More than 10 percent of New Jersey's forest acreage burned that year. In 1936, a wildfire near Tuckerton killed five firefighters and burned over 46,000 acres, and on April 20, 1941, close to 30,000 acres of forest burned in one day. However, the weekend of April 20–22, 1963, under extreme fire danger conditions, when nearly 190,000 acres of forest were destroyed, seven people lost their lives, 2,500 were evacuated, and 1,000 were left homeless, serves as the benchmark for the entire Northeastern United States of what can happen. This chapter will give a flavor of New Jersey wildfires over the past 100 years.

This photograph was taken in the late 1920s of a wildfire that burned between Lakehurst and Toms River. The blazing fire front exceeded 13 miles in length. The photograph was taken by an employee of Aero Service Corporation, flying in a forest fire service monoplane with forest fire pilot Wesley Smith. The photograph later appeared in an article regarding forest firefighting by *Airplane in Aeronautics* magazine in the 1940s. (Photograph by Aero Service Corporation.)

During 1930, 1,620 wildfires burned over 267,547 acres in New Jersey. The average wildfire size for that year was 165 acres. A huge 40,000-acre wildfire during the month of May destroyed a large portion of the town of Forked River. Over 100 buildings were destroyed, and local fire companies from as far away as 30 miles were called in to help protect them. (Photograph by Aero Service Corporation.)

96

This large wildfire is approaching Toms River from the southwest in this c. 1930 photograph. A backfire has been started in the right foreground, along a road, in an attempt to stop the wildfire from reaching the town. Backfiring was common during this time period since mechanized fire equipment was not readily available. (Photograph by Aero Service Corporation.)

This photograph, taken on April 21, 1941, shows a U.S. Navy crew of personnel moving in to assist with firefighting operations near the Lakehurst Navy Base's western boundary. This year a total of 2,472 wildfires burned over 80,769 acres and was the busiest year for the forest fire service since 1930.

The Lakewood Forest Fire of April 20, 1941, destroyed 47 homes, 19 garages, five barns, two chicken coops, and four cars. This photograph shows two homes with flammable shingles being totally consumed by fire. Lakewood had previously adopted a fire-resistant roofing ordinance, and Lakewood fire chief Russell S. Voorhees endorsed the use of asphalt shingles as a fire-resistant house covering. (Photograph by F. W. Tupper.)

This c. 1941 photograph shows a group of firefighters utilizing shovels to extinguish hot spots at the scene of a wildfire in the area of Lakewood, Ocean County. The use of hand tools was very common in the 1940s, as firefighting pumps and trucks were still limited in their availability to the forest fire service and local fire companies. (Photograph by F. W. Tupper.)

The New Lisbon Fire of April 20, 1946, burned 1,065 acres and was caused by a spark from a railroad freight engine on the Pennsylvania Railroad line near New Lisbon. Pictured are two summer homes (one in the foreground and one in the background) that were consumed by the fire. A total of five out of nine homes were destroyed by the fire on the east side of Mount Misery Branch of the Rancocas Creek.

This May 9, 1957, wildfire burned over 900 acres in Jackson Township (Ocean County) and Freehold Township (Monmouth County). This photograph was taken in the afternoon and shows assistant division firewarden Jack Richardson driving through a sheet of flames, just as the fire jumped the road near Jackson Mills. Wildfires had plagued the state for the past two weeks due the lack of rain.

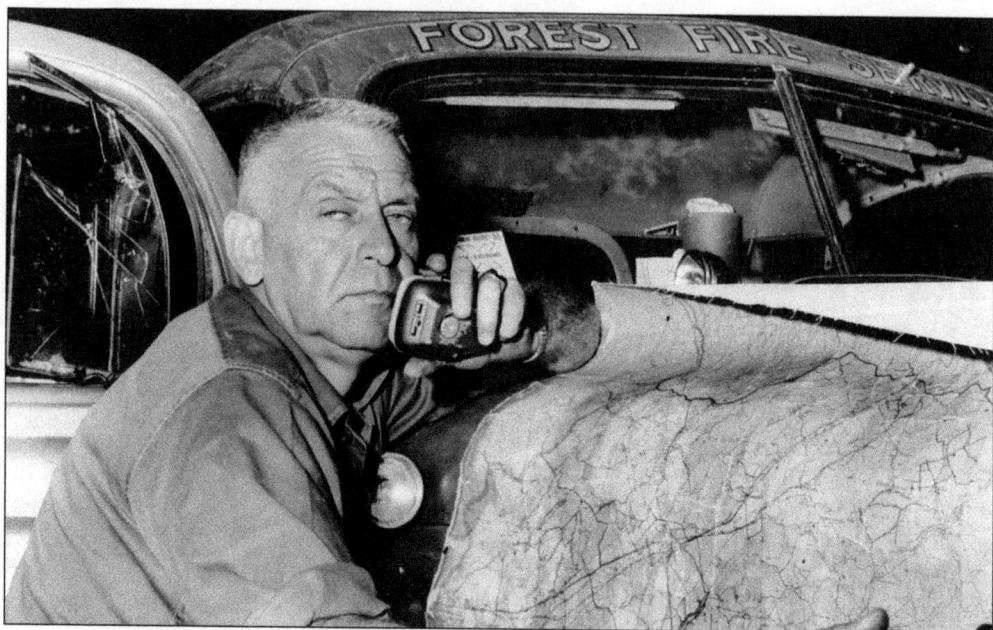

Section firewarden Bill Lance discusses firefighting tactics over the two-way radio after surveying fire line placement on the map and initiating backfires along the north and west side of the fire. This photograph was taken at 1630 hours on September 12, 1964. A note on the back of the photograph explained that fire activity was quite busy over the past week with no sleep possible on September 9, 10, or 11.

Firefighters survey forest fire service Unit A-5 after it turned on its side during rough maneuvering through inaccessible terrain at the Turkey Mountain Fire on September 12, 1964. Only minor injuries were suffered by firewardens operating the Dodge Power Wagon. The unit was quickly set upright and placed back in service with lost fluids replenished and damage to the driver's side door.

This photograph was taken after the great wildfires of April 20, 1963, near Pine Cripple Road on Lebanon State Forest. The area on the left side of the fire line was treated with prescribed fire earlier in the month, and the area on the right of the fire line was not. The area on the right suffered much greater damage from the wildfire. Fifty-four percent of Lebanon State Forest burned during the 1963 fire.

The Chatsworth Wildfire started on July 12, 1954, southwest of Hampton Gate in Shamong Township, Burlington County. By July 13, due to firefighters being hampered by extreme drought conditions, the wildfire quickly spread east and threatened the community of Chatsworth. This photograph shows a home that was destroyed by the fire in Chatsworth. The overall area of the Chatsworth Wildfire was 27,000 acres, with 19,500 acres being burned. Within the fire area, 118 buildings were destroyed with value ranging between $500 and $25,000.

This home was destroyed by wildfire during the weekend of April 20–22, 1963, along Route 72 in Woodland Township, Burlington County. A total of 186 homes were destroyed by wildfire as well as 197 other buildings during this weekend. Buildings included churches, garages, barns, hunting clubs, and saw mills, as well as sheds.

State forester George R. Moorehead and state firewarden William B. Phoenix discuss firefighting strategies after looking at topographic maps in front of the forest fire service mobile fire headquarters bus. Their firefighting discussion concerned the Cologne fire in Atlantic County on April 19, 1971. This early mobile command post was designed to assist forest firewardens with incident command and communications assignments.

New Jersey firefighters carry Bill Donnelly, in a stretcher, across a creek to awaiting emergency medical personnel after being struck in the leg by a large rolling rock. This fire crew was conducting initial attack on a fast spreading wildfire in steep terrain as the fire was dislodging boulders, rocks, and logs, and causing them to roll downhill toward firefighters. The fire crew was assigned to the Steamboat and Fools Hen Wildfire Complexes during the summer of 1989. (Photograph by Willie Cirone.)

Forest fire service firefighters, along with local firefighters, cool down a hot marsh fire to prevent it from crossing East Park Avenue in Pleasantville (Atlantic County) on March 29, 1989. About 25 local residents were evacuated before the wildfire reached 175 acres in size. (Photograph by Whitey Swartz.)

District firewarden Joe Mahoney "rides the hose" as a bombardier pulls thousands of feet of fire hose from the scene of a fire to a location where it can be cleaned and rolled for future use. Firefighters worked the Sawmill Pond Fire in Kinnelon for eight days due to ground fire conditions prior to this photograph being taken on September 19, 1980. Also visible are Mike Drake and Art Labonseur. (Photograph by Kevin Drake.)

This photograph shows how close the Greenwood Wildfire came to hundreds of homes in the Fox Hollow development in Manchester Township on April 4, 1995. Route 539 crosses through the center of the photograph. A bulldozed fire line is clearly visible along the burnt perimeter of the wildfire. This wildfire burned over 19,000 acres and threatened hundreds of homes but destroyed none because of the quick actions of firefighters in protecting threatened homes.

Tractor and plows 304, 305, and 350 await instructions for where to cut fire lines from the incident commander, hovering over the scene in a helicopter, at the Parkdale Wildfire on June 11, 1986. This wildfire burned over 200 acres near Route 206, and firefighting efforts were hampered by shifting winds and temperatures in the 90 degree range. (Photograph by Shirley O'Neill.)

This is a view looking north from Burlington County Road 679 of the Bass River Wildfire moving southwest on April 30, 1999. In the foreground, local cranberry growers have turned on irrigation sprinklers to wet down their bogs in order to protect the cranberry plants. The Bass River Wildfire burned over 11,285 acres of forest.

Assistant division firewarden Jim Mangine prepares a portable pump for a pumping operation from a portable tank during a summer wildfire on Newark Watershed property in Rockaway Township during August 2002. In the left foreground is the edge of a portable tank that holds water for firefighting, and in the background is an aerial view of Charlotteburg Reservoir.

Engine A-7, a Ford F 350, patrols a fire line during a prescribed burning project in Hunterdon County during the winter of 2003. District firewarden Mark O'Grady operates a hose from the crew compartment of the truck while forest fire control technician Scott Knauer drives the engine. Note the trademark armor of the truck developed by the forest fire service to protect the engine when operating in rough and rugged terrain as well as in thick forest vegetation. (Photograph by Willie Cirone.)

On April 4, 1995, the Greenwood Wildfire burned over 19,000 acres of pine barrens forest in Ocean County. This photograph captures the fast spreading wildfire jumping Ocean County Route 539 as forest fire service firefighters watch and size up fire behavior in order to develop a plan of attack. The wildfire was contained the next day, with several hundred homes being threatened during the duration of the wildfire. No homes were destroyed. (Photograph by Kevin Curry.)

Forest fire service firefighters battle a spring wildfire on the steep and rocky terrain of the Kittatinny Ridge in the vicinity of Worthington State Forest in the mid-1990s. In the extreme right portion of the picture, Route 80 is visible several thousand feet below the firefighters.

Section forest firewarden Walter J. Earlin (holding a cranco-style drip torch) discusses the proper technique to light a backfire with Gov. Christine Todd Whitman on scene at the Greenwood Wildfire on April 5, 1995. This wildfire burned over 19,000 acres and was the largest in New Jersey since the Manahawkin Wildfire in 1971, which burned over 21,000 acres. (Photograph by Thomas T. Tansley.)

Section firewarden Steven Holmes (standing in foreground) briefs district firewarden Jim Parker (sitting in the front of canoe) on a plan of attack in attempting to contain the Dover Forge Wildfire on June 8, 1999. At the time of the photograph, the fire was burning near its origin along the Toms River in an Atlantic White Cedar swamp and firefighters used canoes to carry equipment and manpower to the fire scene. Before the fire was controlled, it burned over 278 acres of forest.

This 1998 photograph was taken at a fire-damaged gas station near Titusville, Florida. From left to right are firefighters (first row) Tom Philhower, Jim Garthaus, Artie Grimes, John Carbone, Mike Achey, and Brian Christopher; (second row) Bill Edwards, Steve Holmes, Bill Seeley, John Earlin, Mike Reed, Dave Karpovage, John Tonking, and Kevin Drake.

The Power Plant Wildfire on May 3, 1992, burned over 5,000 acres and threatened the Oyster Creek Nuclear Power Plant in Waretown (Ocean County). This photograph was taken from Route 9 and shows the wildfire getting dangerously close to the power plant. A forest fire service observation helicopter is visible in the air to the right of the fire front.

The crew of B-39 extinguishes a spot fire that was burning in landscape plants and shrubbery before the fire could enter the soffit and attic of a home in the Holiday City development in Berkeley Township, Ocean County, during their response to the Wrangle Brook Wildfire on July 19, 1997.

This photograph captures the Greenwood Wildfire crossing Route 539 in Manchester Township, Ocean County, on April 4, 1995. This photograph is looking south along Route 539 and shows an intense smoke column as the fire is moving southwest pushed by strong northwest winds that accompanied a passing cold front.

Forest fire service engine B–7 cools down a hot spot during the Jakes Branch Wildfire in Berkeley Township, Ocean County, during June 2002. At the time of this photograph, the wildfire threw spot fires and jumped over Grand Central Parkway while destroying one home and damaging several others during this increase in the eastern portion of the wildfire. This portion of the wildfire was eventually contained along Northern Boulevard.

Section firewarden Mike Achey briefs television news reporters during the Goshen Wildfire in Camden County on April 20, 2005. In the background is a forest fire service mobile incident command post that was established to assist in the management of the personnel and equipment assigned to the fire. The fire burned 325 acres of forest land.

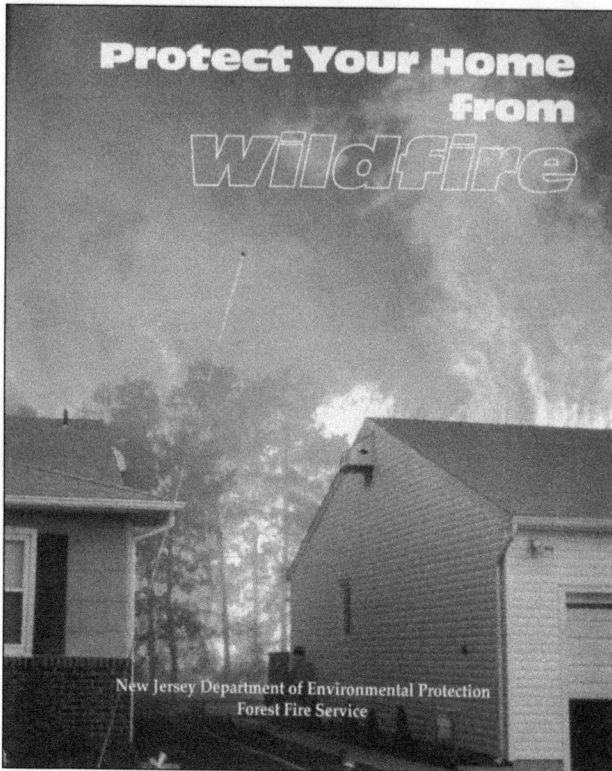

Protect Your Home from Wildfire

New Jersey Department of Environmental Protection
Forest Fire Service

The forest fire service developed a *Protect Your Home from Wildfire* brochure to educate residents and visitors of forest areas that their homes and property can be threatened by wildfire on a yearly basis. The brochure cover shows the July 19, 1997, Wrangle Brook Wildfire spreading closely and threatening several homes in the Holiday City portion of Berkeley Township, Ocean County. This wildfire damaged 52 homes and threatened an additional several hundred homes. (Photograph by Thomas T. Tansley.)

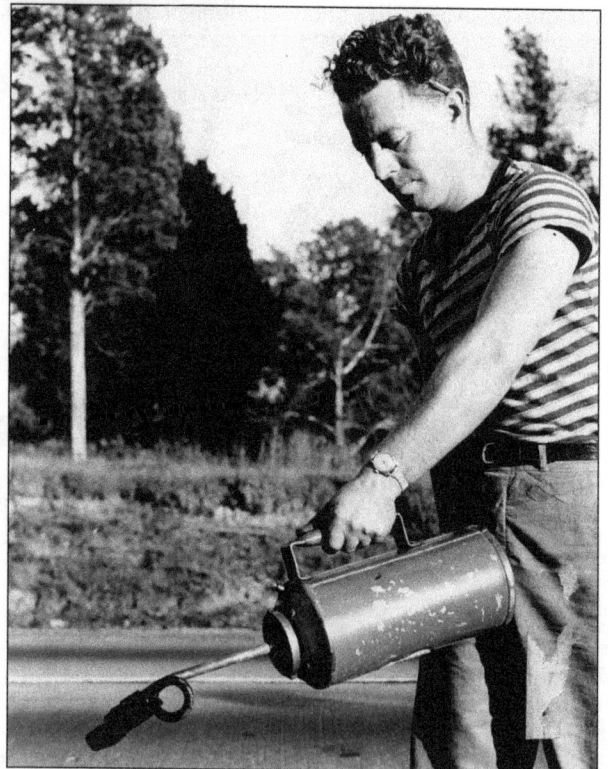

A forest firewarden demonstrates the use of a Forester Seal Tite Backfire Torch in September 1947. This new style torch allows gasoline to pass from the tank through a tube to an asbestos wick that is then ignited. The lighted gasoline then drips on dry leaves and needles and is used to ignite a backfire. In 1947, this model torch was available for purchase from various fire equipment vendors for a price of $12.

Seven

FIRE CACHE

The New Jersey Forest Fire Service has operated within a system of maintaining personnel, tools, vehicles, aircraft, equipment, and supplies that have been assembled in planned quantities at strategic locations across New Jersey since its inception in 1906. This combined cache has made the difference in proactively protecting lives, property, and natural resources from wildfire as well as serving the residents of the state of New Jersey in an effective and cost-efficient manner. This cache goes beyond just firefighting and has included programs such as fire prevention, law enforcement, fire detection, prescribed burning, training, hazard reduction, vehicle research and construction, incident management, and response to other emergencies, as well as emergency vehicle fleet management.

New Jersey has been a leader in the use of prescribed burning as a natural resource management as well as a public-safety tool over its history. Prescribed burning to reduce the build up of hazardous forest vegetation can be traced back to 1914 on private lands and 1928 on state-owned forests. The use of prescribed fire was introduced to the general public in New Jersey in the late 1940s and has been used effectively to create today's overall statewide fire management program.

Fire prevention has been an issue that the forest fire service has had to contend with since the early 20th century. Even back then, due to New Jersey's forested regions being surrounded by dense urban areas, as well as the general public visiting and traversing these areas, nine out of 10 wildfires have historically been caused by humans. Early fire-prevention campaigns include the Junior Forest Fire Assistant in 1917 as well as the embracing of the national forest fire prevention campaign and Smokey Bear in 1944. Today New Jersey's fire prevention program has grown and expanded to include educating the general public on how they can protect their homes and property from wildfire danger.

This chapter takes the opportunity to highlight some of these programs that have been true success stories throughout New Jersey and have promoted the overall positive image of the forest fire service over its first 100 years.

This January 26, 1948, photograph shows the Dodge Power Wagon shop crew in front of the forest fire service repair garage at Bakers Basin Airport. From left to right are Ed Tilley, Austin Maggiloncalda, George Kusnir, Arthur Conover, Bill Staib, and John Salt. The forest fire service purchased its first Dodge Power Wagons for use as off-road engines in 1946.

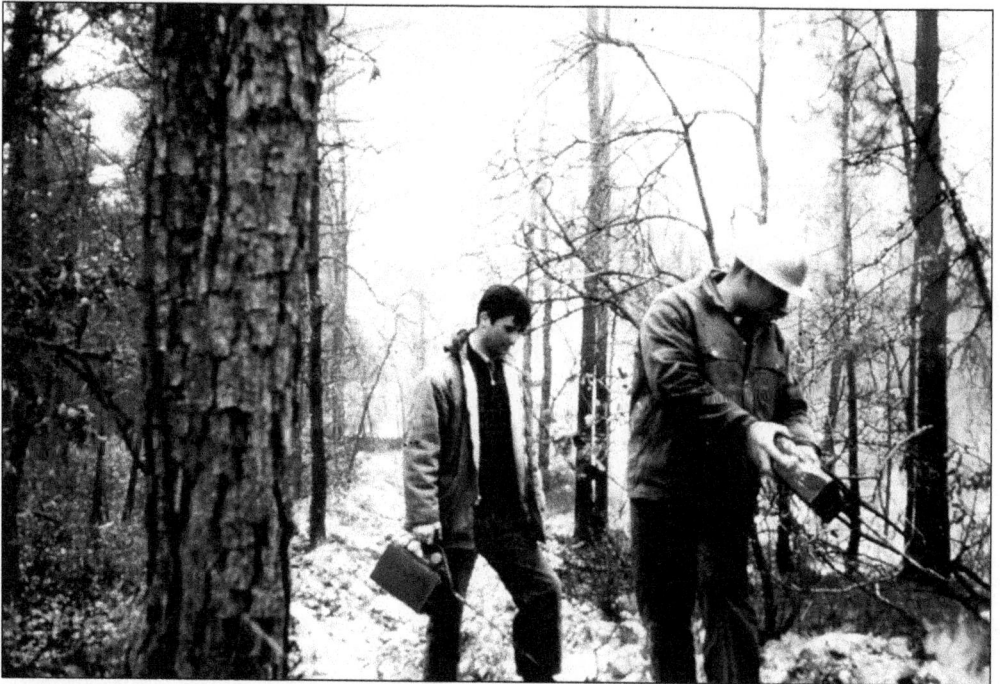

Dave Harrison (right) and John Perry light a plowed line for a prescribed burning project on Wharton State Forest in December 1967. The backfire torches being used are early cranco-style torches that utilized a tin-type can carrying fuel with a detachable wand and handle attached.

In 1991, forest fire service engine C 19 won the title of Best Appearing Brush Truck at the New Jersey State Firemen's Relief Association parade in September. Pictured from left to right are Kenneth Badger Jr., Kenneth Badger Sr. (operator of the truck), division firewarden Carl Owen, and state firewarden Dave Harrison. The off-road engine is a 1979 Dodge Power Wagon and was assigned to Section C-5. (Photograph by Whitey Swartz.)

This 1988 photograph from the Yellowstone wildfires shows members of New Jersey Fire Crew No. 2 enjoying a steak dinner at a makeshift spike camp in a remote section of the Bridger Teton National Forest in Wyoming that August. Looking at the photographer with the aluminum hard hat is crew boss Walter Earlin. In the background of the photograph, spot fires are clearly visible smoldering in a meadow several miles from the main body of the wildfire.

Sectional firewardens from throughout the state met in February 1950 to receive first aid instruction from Harold Bassett of the American Red Cross. This picture shows an explanation of the proper way to apply a leg splint. Firewardens participating included William Seidel, R. Wesley Davis, Peter Crozer, Arthur Conover, Roy Meade, Albert Callahan, Robert Walters, Theodore Holz, Lawrence Terhune, William Phoenix, Calvin Cutts, George Allen, Horace Cook, Joseph Korleski, Frank Kovar, James Cummings, John Brown, and George Post.

Steve Alcorn, standing beside a fire shelter, discusses the safe and proper deployment of a fire shelter at a basic wildland firefighting training course in 2000. Fire shelters have been used by wildland firefighters since 1977. Fire shelters are only utilized as an emergency survival tool in life-threatening situations when a firefighter is unable to escape to a safety zone and is in imminent danger of being burned over by fire.

During the fall of 1987, the forest fire service participated in Operation WILDSAR on portions of Stokes State Forest and the Delaware Water Gap National Recreation Area. The operation was designed to be an exercise to test the capabilities of local, county, state, and federal emergency responders in dealing with a simulated wildfire and simultaneous search for an aircraft that crashed in a remote forested area. This photograph shows firefighters loading up a stretcher with an injured firefighter on engine A–5 in preparation to transport to an awaiting ambulance.

A Dodge Power Wagon off-road engine was the center of attention at the forest fire service display at the 1966 Trenton State Fair. The display demonstrates how the engine can do a mobile attack on a wildfire through thick forest vegetation and shows how a firefighter would stand behind the cab of the engine and spray water at the flames as the driver encircled the fire.

A forest fire service display at the 1946 Trenton State Fair highlights a state-of-the-art tractor and fire plow unit. This display demonstrates how a tractor unit can cut a fire line along the side fire of a large wildfire and prevent the fire from spreading. This tractor and plow unit was considered experimental in 1946 and was credited in preventing an additional 3,000 acres of forest from being destroyed at six large wildfires.

The New Jersey Forest Fire Service has historically participated in regional and local parades. In 1956, forest firewardens from Division A participated along with Smokey Bear at the Budd Lake Volunteer Fire Department's 75th Anniversary parade. The first unit (with Smokey) is a World War II surplus Jeep, the second unit is a 1939 Ford cab over engine, and the third is a Dodge WM 300 Power Wagon. (Photograph by George Baumann.)

This tin sign from the 1960s exclaims a fire prevention message but also clarifies the state forest fire laws regarding the requirement of obtaining a fire permit for all open fires as well as a mandatory notification to a firewarden of any wildfire. This type of sign was very commonly posted by forest firewardens on trees and utility poles along well-traveled roads throughout the forested regions of New Jersey.

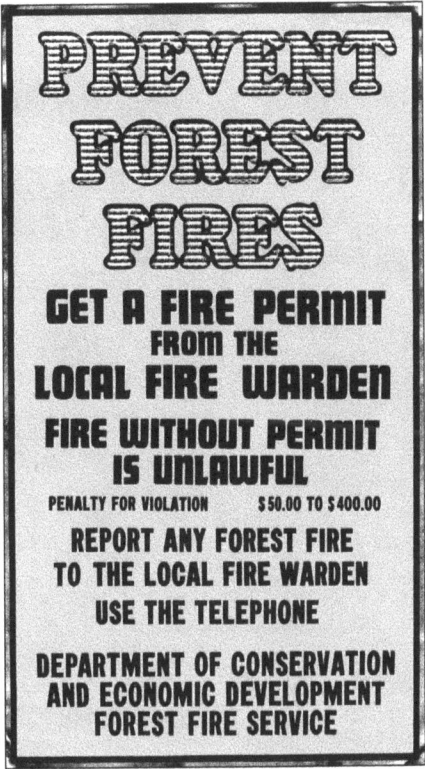

PREVENT FOREST FIRES

GET A FIRE PERMIT
FROM THE
LOCAL FIRE WARDEN
FIRE WITHOUT PERMIT
IS UNLAWFUL
PENALTY FOR VIOLATION $50.00 TO $400.00
REPORT ANY FOREST FIRE
TO THE LOCAL FIRE WARDEN
USE THE TELEPHONE

DEPARTMENT OF CONSERVATION
AND ECONOMIC DEVELOPMENT
FOREST FIRE SERVICE

In 1984, Smokey Bear celebrated his 40th birthday across the United States by way of a caravan that transported Smokey between all 50 states. Here Smokey Bear arrives at Liberty State Park by way of a New Jersey Forest Fire Service engine in preparation of being transported into New York City by way of a fire boat. Assistant division firewarden Phil Hockenberry is accompanying Smokey on the back of the fire engine.

Smokey Bear attended the 1969 fire prevention week parade at Sears Town Mall in Egg Harbor Township (Atlantic County). Pictured from left to right are Stanley Kwasnieski, Ken Badger, Gene Stetser as Smokey, Carl Owen, and Arnold Liepe.

Conservation commissioner Erdman presented Governor Driscoll with a Smokey Bear doll to launch a new Smokey Bear junior forest ranger program in cooperation with the U.S. Forest Service on October 8, 1953, at the state house in Trenton. The program would recruit a corps of junior forest rangers that would help prevent forest fires and protect New Jersey's forests, wildlife, and other natural resources. Pictured from left to right are Andrew G. Brenneis of the U.S. Forest Service; R. Wesley Davis, assistant state firewarden; Commissioner Erdman; William J. Seidel, state firewarden; and Governor Driscoll. (Photograph by M. W. Barish.)

This 1960s-era traveling fire-prevention display was used by the forest fire service to spread Smokey Bear's fire-prevention message. This display allowed children as well as adults to have their photograph taken with Smokey and also be considered as "Champion" forest fire preventers by Smokey Bear and the New Jersey Forest Fire Service. Several Boy Scouts and their leader exchange a laugh as they discuss Smokey's message.

This poster appeared as a pull-out centerpiece of a *New Jersey Outdoors* magazine in 1989. The poster captures Smokey Bear with comedian Dom Deluise spreading a wildfire awareness message to residents of New Jersey's forested regions. The message targets forest homeowners and advises them to take precautions to make their home and property less vulnerable to the threat of wildfire.

A Clarkaire dozer with plow is plowing a side fire on March 9, 1949, in the New Jersey Pine Barrens. The plow cuts a 36-inch-wide fire line in the earth down to mineral soil. This plow is capable of cutting through the roots of trees and shrubs.

The c. 1951 photograph shows a demonstration of firefighting equipment at Camp Wapalanna in Stokes State Forest in Sussex County. The demonstration included the operation of fire engines as well as the use of backpack Indian brand fire tanks. The young ladies in the photograph are testing Indian fire pumps and had stated that the equipment was easy to use and lots of fun. State firewarden William Seidel is in the right foreground of the photograph.

This 1950s photograph shows Lakewood Lookout Tower on Massachusetts Avenue in Lakewood. The tower is located on the highest point in Ocean County and offers a commanding view of Ocean and Monmouth Counties. On a clear day, the New York City skyline is visible, as well as large container ships in the shipping channels in the Atlantic Ocean. In the foreground is a Jeep pick-up truck that was used by staff firewardens from the Division B office.

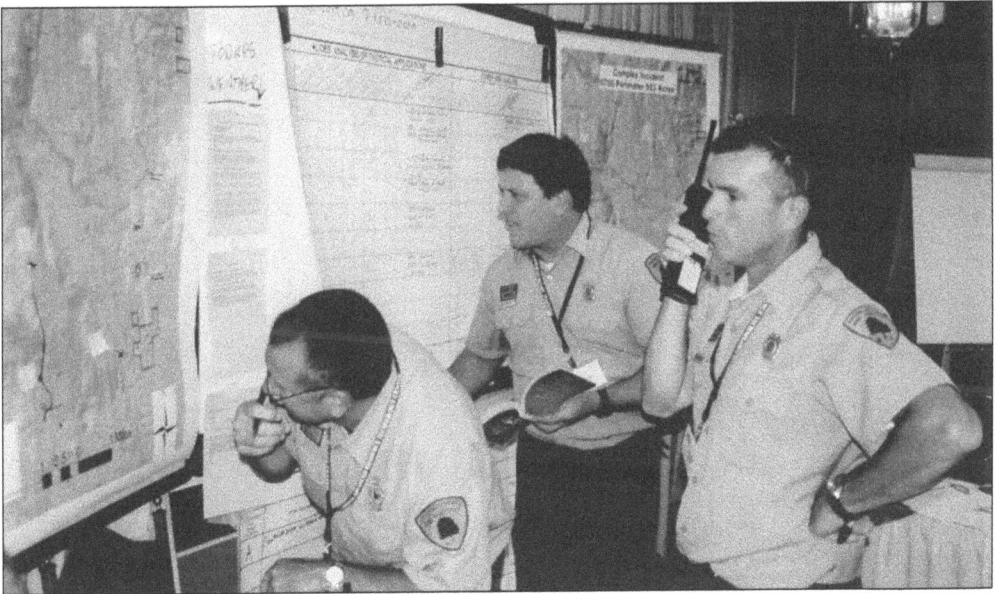

Members of the New Jersey Forest Fire Service Complex Incident Management Team participate in an all-day incident management exercise in 2005. The National Association of State Foresters sponsored training is designed to instruct and certify state forestry agency incident management teams from across the United States. From left to right, information officer Glenn Liepe, incident commander Mike Drake, and operations section chief Thomas Gerber review maps and discuss incident management strategies.

Section forest firewarden William H. Hagerthy utilizes a two-way radio in his fire engine to discuss firefighting strategies with adjoining firefighters on March 9, 1949, near Vincentown, Burlington County. The availability of two radios in fire trucks greatly improved communications as well as safety for all firefighters on the fire line.

This March 16, 1949, image captures section forest firewarden Carlton Taylor sitting in the driver's seat of his 1940s vintage fire truck, awaiting the report of a wildfire. In the background is Medford Fire Tower located in Medford Township, Burlington County. At the first sighting of smoke from a possible wildfire, the lookout tower observer would immediately notify the firewarden of the possible fire to ensure a quick attack of all wildfires.

This color guard led a complement of forest fire service marchers and equipment that participated in the 128th Annual New Jersey State Firemen's Convention and parade in September 2005. The color guard consisted of Russell Fenton, Edward Lord Jr., William Love, David Achey, Shawn Judy, Michael Achey Jr., and Kenneth Badger Jr. The banner celebrates the centennial of the forest fire service and highlights the mission of protecting lives, property, and natural resources since 1906. (Photograph by Jim Petrini.)

On September 17, 2005, the New Jersey Forest Fire Service kicked off its centennial celebration by participating in the New Jersey State Firemen's Association 128th Annual Convention and parade. The 1969 WM model Dodge Power leads the forest fire service contingent of vehicles and marchers. The Power Wagon was restored specifically for the centennial, and this was its grand appearance. Also visible on the Power Wagon is Smokey Bear, who is the national symbol for forest fire prevention. (Photograph by Jim Petrini.)

New Jersey Forest Fire Service
State Firewardens

13.9-13 – The State Firewarden, under the direction of the Commissioner, shall administer and supervise the Forest Fire Service, cooperating agencies, and such laws as shall deal with the protection of forests, from wildfire.

Theophilus P. Price	1906 – 1910
Charles P. Wilber	1910 – 1923
Leonidas Coyle	1923 – 1937
LeRoy S. Fales	1937 – 1944
William J. Seidel	1944 – 1960
R. Wesley Davis	1960 – 1968
William B. Phoenix	1968 – 1975
James A. Cumming Jr.	1975 – 1982
David B. Harrison	1982 – 2001
Maris G. Gabliks	2001 - current

During the last 100 years, 10 individuals have served in the leadership position of state firewarden of the New Jersey Forest Fire Service. Their names and dates of service are listed above.

In Memoriam
Firefighters Killed in the Line of Duty
While Fighting New Jersey Wildfires

John T. LaSalle	May 26, 1936	Civilian Conservation Corps
Edward F. Sullivan	May 26, 1936	Civilian Conservation Corps
Stanley Carr	May 26, 1936	Civilian Conservation Corps
Kingsley White	May 26, 1936	Forest Fire Service
Ira Morey	May 26, 1936	Forest Fire Service
Carl Luderitz	March 27, 1943	Forest Fire Service
William Hoover	April 5, 1943	Forest Fire Service
Alfred Ingersoll	March 26, 1943	Forest Fire Service
Ralph Luderitz	March 26, 1943	Forest Fire Service
George Herbert	April 10, 1955	Forest Fire Service
Marcus P. Cullen, Jr.	July 22, 1977	Eagleswood Fire Company
John F. Baker	July 22, 1977	Eagleswood Fire Company
Herbert E. Blackwell	July 22, 1977	Eagleswood Fire Company
Harold E. Cranmer, Jr.	July 22, 1977	Eagleswood Fire Company

Wildland firefighters are the backbone of an effective forest fire management and wildfire protection program. Their job can be very demanding and dangerous under constantly changing wildfire conditions. During the past 100 years, 14 firefighters have died in the line of duty directly battling wildfires in the protection of lives, property, and New Jersey's natural resources.

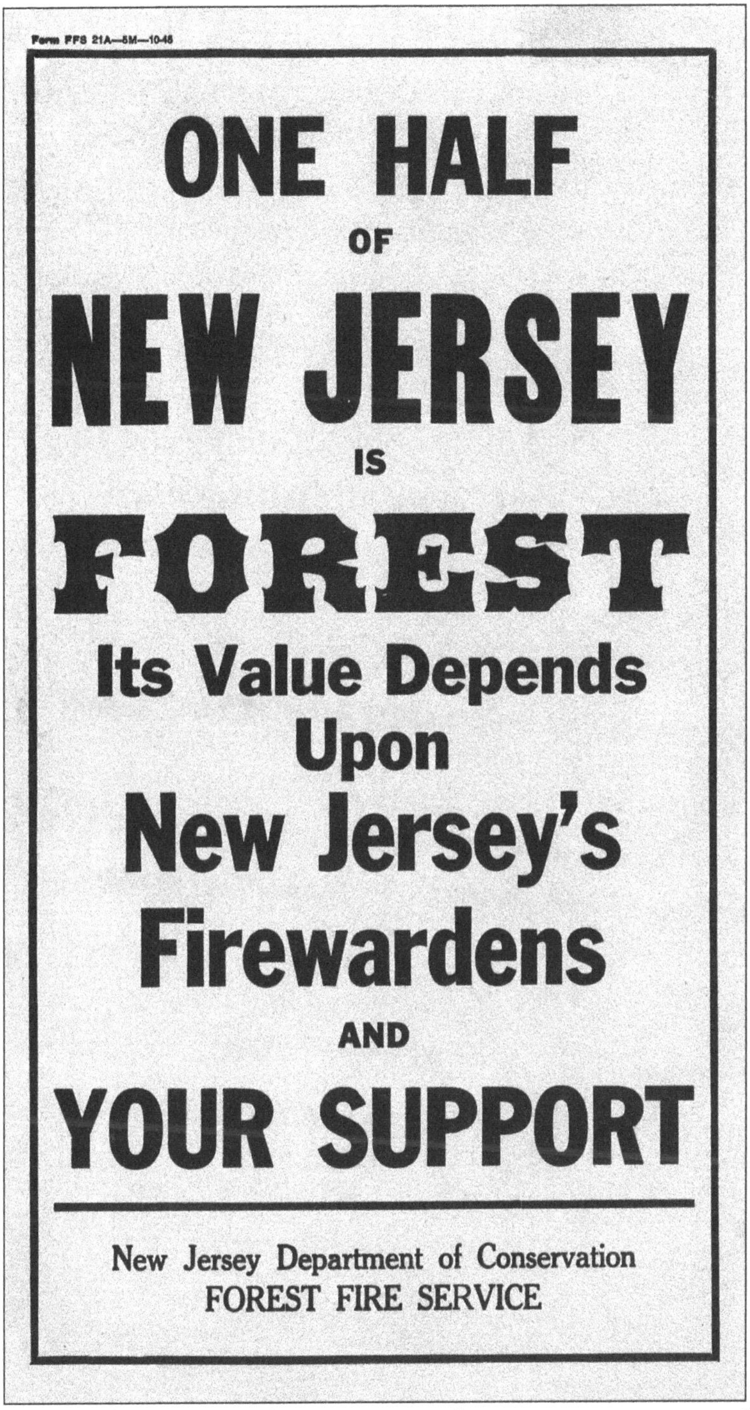

ONE HALF

OF

NEW JERSEY

IS

FOREST

Its Value Depends

Upon

New Jersey's

Firewardens

AND

YOUR SUPPORT

New Jersey Department of Conservation
FOREST FIRE SERVICE

This poster was utilized by the forest fire service as a tool to promote an awareness of wildfires in New Jersey as well as to publicize the importance of firewardens in 1945. Historically the forest fire service has been comprised of a combination of permanent and part-time on-call forest firewardens. Local firewardens have always been an important part of their communities, and this awareness campaign helped raise an awareness of their important mission.

Discover Thousands of Local History Books Featuring Millions of Vintage Images

Arcadia Publishing, the leading local history publisher in the United States, is committed to making history accessible and meaningful through publishing books that celebrate and preserve the heritage of America's people and places.

Find more books like this at
www.arcadiapublishing.com

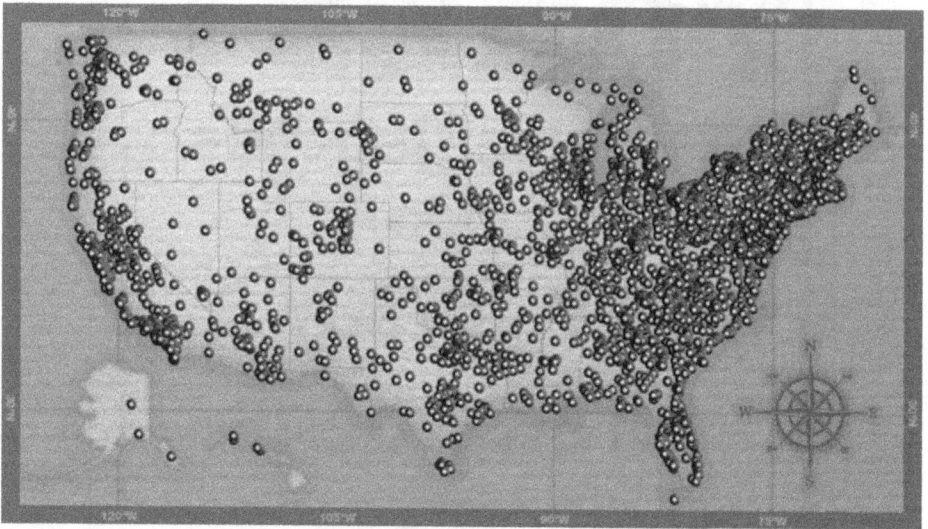

Search for your hometown history, your old stomping grounds, and even your favorite sports team.

www.ingramcontent.com/pod-product-compliance
Lightning Source LLC
Chambersburg PA
CBHW050705110426
42813CB00007B/2090